36 DEVOTIONALS
FOR WOMEN'S GROUPS

by Idalee Vonk

STANDARD PUBLISHING
Cincinnati, Ohio

3216

To Burney
A Kindred Spirit

Library of Congress Catalog Number: 81-52993

ISBN: 0-87239-493-X

Introduction

During my life I have been blessed with many and varied opportunities out of which have come many and varied experiences. Some
of these I have incorporated in this book of devotions for women.

Born, reared, and educated in Cincinnati, Ohio, I was employed
for four years by the Standard Publishing Company. I left that position to become Publicity Director of the Cleveland Christian Home
for Children. In 1941, I resigned that position to marry Paul Kenneth
Vonk, then working on his Ph.D. in Philosophy at Duke University.

During World War II, I managed my father-in-law's wallpaper,
paint, and decorating business in Grand Rapids, Michigan, as his
health was failing and my husband was a Lieutenant Commander
serving in the Aleutians, the South Pacific, and Europe.

After the war, I earned both Bachelor and Master degrees in education at the University of Miami, and subsequently taught elementary grades in both public and private schools in Dade County,
Florida.

While my husband was Vice President for Academic Affairs at the
University of West Florida, Pensacola, during the organizational
stages of that institution of higher education, I was a reading super-
visor for Escambia County, planned and directed a Developmental
Reading Program at the Center for Adult Studies, Pensacola Junior
College, and was appointed adjunct professor for both Florida State
University and the University of South Florida, teaching graduate
students (elementary and high-school teachers) in the field of reading.

During the last ten years of my teaching career, I taught various
professional courses in the School of Education on two campuses,
preparing students to become elementary teachers.

Throughout our thirty-five years of academe, I have had the
privilege of sharing in my husband's career as he filled, in sequence,
the positions of Associate Professor of Philosophy, Professor of Philosophy, Director of Honors Program, Assistant Dean of the College
of Arts and Sciences, Dean of University College at the University of
Miami; Vice President for Academic Affairs at two universities; and
President of Oglethorpe University, Atlanta, for eight years. In June,
1975, he retired and was named President Emeritus. After a three
months' retirement, he was invited to assume responsibilities as

Holder of the James D. Compton Chair for the Study of Private Enterprise, Brunswick College.

Our daughter, Claire, earned a Ph.D. in Political Science and is a C.P.A. She is married to Gary H. Brooks, also a Ph.D. in Political Science, now teaching at the University of Arkansas, Little Rock. Our son, Paul Kenneth, is a member of the Georgia Bar.

It was my hope in preparing these devotions that some of my experiences might not only be of interest but of inspiration, for truly there are "sermons in stones" and evidences of God's great love for us in our everyday lives, if we but train our eyes to see such blessings.

—Idalee Vonk

Contents

Dove Cote or Pigeon Coop

The hearing ear, and the seeing eye, the Lord hath made even both of them (Proverbs 20:12).

~~~~~~

Opening Meditation

O God, who dost know our strengths
    as well as our weaknesses;
Our spoken words
    as well as our secret thoughts;
Our noble aspirations
    inspired by unselfishness
As well as our ambitions
    motivated by selfish desires;
Help us, we pray, so we may live each day
    according to Your high precepts.
Open our eyes so we may see
    all the beauty surrounding us.
Open our ears so we may hear
    all the joyous sounds of life.
And slow us down, Lord, so we have time
    to hear the birds,
    to see the sunsets,
    and to smell the flowers.

Opening Hymn: Open My Eyes

Devotional

A group of tourists were being conducted through a recently restored home in a charming historical city in south Georgia. When the tour ended, the guide invited them to step out of the kitchen door and into a little backyard garden. About ten feet from the house stood a small wooden structure. Pointing to it, the guide said, "That's a dove cote or a pigeon coop; it's all in how you look at it."

A dove cote or a pigeon coop. What contrasting pictures flash across our minds!

A dove cote. A picturesque structure housing cooing, gentle doves which, since Biblical times, have been the symbol of peace and tranquility.

7

A pigeon coop. An ordinary wooden box built on stilts, and housing noisy, bothersome pigeons, carriers of multi-disease germs.

So often in everyday life we have opportunities, especially with children and young people, to create a mental picture by our choice of words. We can create either dove cotes or pigeon coops. We can look at an object or a situation and, by our choice of words, brand it beautiful or unsightly, important or mundane. When we see only pigeon coops, we miss much of life's beauty.

As we live, so we think. As we think, so we speak. As we speak, we encourage or discourage, motivate or stifle, inspire or dispirit. Through our example, we reveal God's love or miss daily opportunities to witness for Christ through all aspects of our lives.

Margaret Fuller, editor and author, wrote, "There is in every creature a fountain of life, which, if not choked back by stones and other dead rubbish, will create a fresh atmosphere, and bring to life beauty."

When we train our eyes to see dove cotes, we perpetuate the flame of beauty within ourselves and ignite the flame of beauty in those about us.

Closing Hymn: All the Way My Savior Leads Me

Closing Thought

A kind word is never lost,
But rather is twice blessed.
It blesses her who sends it on its way
And also blesses the recipient.
Kind words reveal our thoughts
And, like a mirror,
Reflect our hearts and souls.
Speaking a kind word is like making
A good investment.
The returns profit many,
But none more than the one
Who first sent the kind word on its way.

The Meaning of the Holy Spirit

I will pray the Father, and he shall give you another Comforter, that he may abide with you for ever. But the Comforter, which is the Holy Ghost, whom the Father will send in my name, he shall teach you all things, and bring all things to your remembrance, whatsoever I have said unto you (John 14:16, 26).

∿∿∿∿∿∿∿∿∿∿∿∿∿∿∿∿∿∿∿∿∿∿∿∿∿∿∿∿∿∿

Opening Meditation

In Thee, O Lord, do I put my trust; let me never be ashamed: deliver me in thy righteousness.

Bow down thine ear to me; deliver me speedily: be thou my strong rock, for a house of defense to save me.

For thou art my rock and my fortress; therefore for thy name's sake lead me, and guide me.

Pull me out of the net that they have laid privily for me: for thou art my strength.

Into thine hand I commit my spirit: thou hast redeemed me, O Lord God of truth *(Psalm 31:1-5).*

Opening Hymn: Holy Spirit, With Light Divine

Devotional

Most little girls like pretty ribbons. One afternoon, little Idalee was walking home from her grandmother's house, clutching a treasured bag of ribbons and bows, when two older boys jumped out of a doorway and screamed at her. They meant no harm. It was just a boyish prank intended to frighten her. But to a small, scrawny five-year-old, they were two monsters. Idalee was too frightened to scream, but much to the boys' delight, she was petrified. The boys kept prancing in front of her, facing her as she tried to avoid them, blocking the sidewalk at every turn.

Completely shaken, little Idalee turned around and ran as fast as she could back to the corner, down that short block and turned the next corner, intending to take that route home. Of course, the boys knew what she was planning. When she reached the back of their home, they were waiting for her with the same treatment.

The little girl could think of nothing else to do but to repeat the procedure. She turned, ran as fast as she could to the corner, around the corner, and back to the main street. But there were the boys waiting for her in the doorway. She began to cry, feeling all was lost, when suddenly, she saw a man walking by himself in front of her. Just as he started across the sidewalk in front of the boys, she quickened her steps and walked close to him, keeping near the street side of the pavement. Idalee kept hurrying along by the side of the man, taking three steps to every one of his, until they were well past the boys. Then she ran as fast as she could the rest of the way home.

Many children, and adults as well, are confused by the term, "Father, Son, and Holy Ghost." Father and Son are not particularly difficult, for we understand the earthly father-son relationship. It is the Holy Ghost that troubles us; we cannot conceive of ever wanting to be close to a ghost, not even a holy one.

If we use the word *Spirit* for *Ghost,* it may help somewhat. But we need to go a little farther in our understanding of how the Spirit works in our lives before we can appreciate the gift of the Holy Spirit. The Holy Spirit can be with us always, no matter where we are or what the occasion. He will give us strength, patience, and wisdom, filling whatever need we may have at any given time. The Holy Spirit is like a silent friend who walks beside us, giving us courage to face difficult tasks.

It's like the experience of the little girl with the two boys—except better.

The Holy Spirit is available at all times to everyone, but every individual has to personally want to walk with Him—to walk beside Him. When we choose to do that, He provides the same courage and strength the little girl received from the stranger because she chose to walk close to him.

Closing Hymn: Take the Name of Jesus

Closing Thought

The eternal God is thy refuge, and underneath are the everlasting arms *(Deuteronomy 33:27).*

Seeing Beyond the Obvious

For he saith to Moses, I will have mercy on whom I will have mercy, and I will have compassion on whom I will have compassion (Romans 9:15).

~~~~~~

Opening Meditation

> A truly great heart is one filled with
>   compassion for fellowmen.
> Edmund Spenser wrote,
>   "Who will not mercie unto others shew,
>   How can he mercie ever hope to have?"
> In the Sermon on the Mount, Jesus said,
>   Blessed are the merciful:
>   for they shall obtain mercy *(Matthew 5:7).*
> Woe unto you, scribes and Pharisees, hypocrites!
>   for ye pay tithe of mint and anise and cummin,
>   and have omitted the weightier matters of the law,
>   judgment, mercy, and faith:
>   these ought ye to have done,
>   and not to leave the other undone *(Matthew 23:23).*
> A truly great heart is one filled with
>   compassion for fellowmen.

Opening Hymn: Beneath the Cross of Jesus

Devotional

Idalee walked to Sunday school every Sunday with her sisters and brothers. And every Sunday they stopped by on the way home from church to visit their grandparents and two aunts. The highlight of their weekly visits for Idalee was the privilege of holding Mary Ann, an aunt's childhood doll. Mary Ann, in her blue calico dress trimmed with red braid and her unbleached muslin undergarments, was the most beautiful thing Idalee had ever seen.

In time, the family moved away, the children became teenagers, and Idalee forgot all about Mary Ann. Then one day when Idalee was grown, her aunt presented her with a present. It was the beloved Mary Ann. But what a surprise!

"What—what happened to Mary Ann?" the grown-up girl asked

in distress, amazement, disappointment, and compassion. "Her right hand is missing!"

It was the aunt's turn to look astounded.

"Honey, her hand always has been missing. She was not a new doll when she was given to me as a child, and her right hand was missing then."

All those years the little girl had carried Mary Ann so tenderly every Sunday without noticing the missing hand!

Physical defects are easily overlooked when tenderness, love, and devotion are part of our nature. But such compassionate traits must be acquired. We have all seen how cruel children can be to a child who has a slight physical deviation. It is not that children are cruel by nature. It is simply that they have not lived long enough to develop their personalities and judgment to the extent that they can display tenderness, understanding, compassion, and love to the fullest degree in all situations.

Their eyes see only the obvious. They have not had the time or experience necessary to train their eyes to penetrate beyond the obvious and see the individual behind the defect. Unfortunately, some young people and adults never mature in this respect.

Each one of us has defects—deficiencies—deviations of some kind and to varying degrees. A physician once said he would have to examine over a million people to find a truly perfect specimen. It behooves us not only to work continually on developing and enlarging our own sensitivity toward the feelings of others; we must go out of our way to help every child associated with our lives to do likewise. This is a most positive way to live a prayer of thanks for the many blessings with which each of us has been endowed and to acknowledge our continuing need for the mercy and understanding of God.

John Greenleaf Whittier summed these thoughts by writing, "The sooner we recognize the fact that the mercy of the All-Merciful extends to every creature endowed with life, the better it will be for us as men and Christians."

In one short sentence, William Cowper gives us a revealing picture of the endless mercy of God: "Man may dismiss compassion from the heart, but God never will."

In like manner, Jeremy Taylor paints for us a word picture with a deep and significant meaning: "Mercy is like the rainbow which God hath set in the clouds; it never shines after it is night. If we refuse to show mercy here, we shall receive justice in eternity."

Closing Hymn: Make Me a Blessing

Closing Thought

Finally, be ye all of one mind, having compassion one of another; love as brethren, be pitiful, be courteous:

Not rendering evil for evil, or railing for railing: but contrariwise blessing; knowing that ye are thereunto called, that ye should inherit a blessing *(1 Peter 3:8, 9).*

Time Out for Solitude

And in the morning, rising up a great while before day, he [Jesus] went out, and departed into a solitary place, and there prayed (Mark 1:35).

∧∧∧

Opening Meditation

Can you feel the presence of God when you are alone
With a minute or an hour to devote to solitude?
Can you hear His gentle voice?
Can you see His patient smile?
Can you feel His hand upon your shoulder, relaxing your body,
    filling it with peace?
Filling your mind with ease?
Filling your heart with hope?
If you can, then come, and once again sense His presence close to
    you even though you are one of a group.
If you can't, then come and meet the Lord, your God, who is here
    waiting for you at this place in this hour.

Opening Hymn: Sweet Hour of Prayer

Devotional

A favorite game at children's parties is Shoot the Bull's-eye. Each one toes a chalk line, closes one eye, sights the bull's-eye with the other eye, aims the gun, and pulls the trigger that sends a cork toward the target.

One by one the children had had a turn at shooting the gun, but none had come anywhere near the target. When it was finally Idalee's turn, to her dismay, she discovered she could not close one eye without the other eye closing also. No matter how hard she tried, she could not keep one eye open and the other eye closed without using one hand to cover one eye—and she needed both hands to hold the gun and pull the trigger. Finally, out of despair, Idalee closed both eyes, held the gun as steadily as she could, pulled the trigger—and hit the bull's-eye squarely in the center.

There are times in each life when it is necessary to close both eyes and blot out everything in sight in order to think more clearly, to get a better grip of oneself, to evaluate goals, to regain a balanced perspective in order to make the right choice or decision. The more distractions and confusion that surround us, the greater the need to slip away by ourselves for a period of quiet meditation.

Such moments are essential in every life. We all need moments to relax, to know ourselves. But of even greater importance, we all need moments to seek God and find Him anew.

Emerson wrote, "To go into solitude, a man needs to retire as much from his chamber as from society."

H. D. Thoreau, one of Emerson's contemporaries, expressed his belief in the importance of time for solitude in each life by explaining that he had three chairs in his house: "one for solitude, two for friendship, three for company."

According to Bruce Barton, "It would do the world good if every man in it would compel himself occasionally to be absolutely alone. Most of the world's progress has come out of such solitude."

The Power of Solitude
In solitude the mind regains true convictions,
The heart regains increased courage,
The soul regains deep inner peace,
The body regains added strength
If we spend the precious moments of solitude
In the presence of God.

Closing Hymn: Let Jesus Come Into Your Heart

Closing Thought

In solitude the mind gains strength
And learns to lean upon itself and God.
—*Anonymous*

The Blessings of a Conscience

And ye shall know the truth, and the truth shall make you free (John 8:32).

~~~~~~

Opening Meditation

It is easy to get swept along with the tide of everyday living,
To become too involved with acquiring worldly possessions,
To drift along with the current trends or popular notions;
Turning deafened ears to our consciences,
Turning blinded eyes to the consequences of our acts,
Steeling our hearts when making decisions between
    what we want to do and
    what we know is right.
But the true follower of Christ tunes her ears to
    the voice of her conscience and
    conscientiously studies the Word of God;
For our consciences tell us that we ought to do right,
But the Word of God tells us what is the right thing to do.

Opening Hymn: Yield Not to Temptation

Prayer

Devotional

A third grader copied an essay word-for-word from a library book, signed her name to it, handed it in, and rejoiced over the praise she received from her teacher, never realizing she had done something wrong.

In making the assignment, the teacher had given each child in the class the name of a different bird and said, "Go to the library, find a book that tells about your bird, and write an essay. You will find all the information you need written right in the book"—or words to that general effect.

Of course, what the teacher meant was for the child to read that portion of the book devoted to her particular bird and then write an essay in her own words— to paraphrase what she had read. But the teacher failed to make herself clear, at least to Idalee. Since this was the first time Idalee had been given an assignment like this, she thought she was following the instructions most carefully.

16

Idalee was assigned the catbird. So, obediently, she went to the libary after school, located a book telling about the catbird, and proceeded to painstakingly copy word-for-word from the book. Her aim was to make an exact copy since, by so doing, she would be pleasing her teacher. The teacher was so delighted with Idalee's essay, she sent her across the hall to read it to the other third-grade class after she had read it to her classmates. That day Idalee basked in an undeserved shower of praise.

It was not until the following year when her fourth-grade teacher gave the class a similar assignment that Idalee realized what she had done. This time, the teacher carefully explained that it was perfectly honest to use someone else's thoughts when the students looked up material on a subject in the libary, but it was dishonest to use some-one else's exact words in an essay without giving credit to the person who wrote them.

Until that day, each time Idalee saw her third-grade teacher monitoring the hall at the door of her classroom, she would smile brightly—a smile revealing childish love and adoration for a teacher. After that day, Idalee could no longer look her in the eye.

Conscience is a wonderful mechanism that keeps us on the right track. A lie detector that bars our attempts to deceive. A concealed alarm system that alerts us to our true motives.

Two ancient Greek proverbs remind us that *A healthy conscience is like a wall of brass,* and *Conscience chastises the soul.*

According to H. C. Trumbull, "Conscience tells us that we ought to do right, but it does not tell us what right is—that we are taught by God's Word."

The poet Byron regarded conscience as "the oracle of God."

Frances Bowen described conscience as "a divine voice in the human soul." H. L. Mencken defined it as "an inner voice that warns us somebody is looking."

Closing Hymn: Savior, Like a Shepherd Lead Us

Closing Thought

The Eyes of God

All-seeing eyes: The eyes of the Lord are in every place, beholding the evil and the good (Proverbs 15:3).

Penetrating eyes: All things are naked and opened unto the eyes of him with whom we have to do (Hebrews 4:13).

Thoughtful eyes: For the ways of man are before the eyes of the Lord, and he pondereth all his goings (Proverbs 5:21).

Remembering eyes: And they consider not in their hearts that I remember all their wickedness: now their own doings have beset them about; they are before my face (Hosea 7:2).

Judging eyes: Thine eyes are open upon all the ways of the sons of men, to give every one according to his ways, and according to the fruit of his doings (Jeremiah 32:19).

Providing eyes: A land which the Lord thy God careth for: the eyes of the Lord thy God are always upon it, from the beginning of the year even unto the end of the year (Deuteronomy 11:12).

—*Anonymous*

The Right Word at the Right Time

Let the words of my mouth, and the meditation of my heart, be acceptable in thy sight, O Lord, my strength, and my redeemer (Psalm 19:14).

~~~~~~

Opening Meditation

Come, ye children, hearken unto me: I will teach you the fear of the Lord.
Keep thy tongue from evil, and thy lips from speaking guile.
Depart from evil, and do good; seek peace, and pursue it.
The eyes of the Lord are upon the righteous, and his ears are open unto their cry (*Psalm 34:11, 13-15*).

Opening Hymn: Come, Thou Fount of Every Blessing

Devotional

There was a time when being able to skillfully manipulate a yo-yo was considered the height of achievement among school children. Another time the dexterity with which one could maneuver a hula hoop decided his position among his peers.

When Idalee was in the fourth grade, peer recognition was acquired by being able to place a tiny lilac bloom in each joint of all four fingers and the thumb of the left hand if you were right-handed, and the right hand if you were left-handed.

Lilac season was half over, and only one boy in the class had achieved this remarkable accomplishment. The rest of the class kept trying, vainly. They would carefully pluck the tiny individual blooms from the cluster forming the cone-shaped blossoms, being very careful not to detach the fragile stem connecting each little bloom. Then, with painstaking effort, they would bend each finger, one joint at a time, place the tiny stem in the knuckle crease and carefully straighten the finger.

If one did everything exactly right, the tiny purple or white floweret would stand erect, being held securely by the now closed crease in the skin over the finger joint. This is a most difficult stunt, as it requires a high degree of muscular control. (Try it sometime.)

Well, one balmy May afternoon, Idalee sat during the arithmetic lesson with her hands well under her desk and the bisected lilac bloom in her desk. And, instead of giving her undivided attention to the problems being solved on the blackboard by various students, Idalee aspired to be the first girl to accomplish the lilac feat.

Perhaps it was the playful spring breezes that danced through the open windows filling the room with a feeling of complete relaxation, or maybe Idalee had tried so hard so long that she had, little by little, gained the necessary control over each joint of each finger. Whatever the reason, that afternoon for the first (and last) time in her life, Idalee succeeded in having nine tiny flowerets stand erect in the eight joints of her four fingers and the one joint of her thumb on her left hand.

She was elated beyond words. But the afternoon was only half over, and she could not keep her hand immobilized until after school to proudly show her peers. Idalee's impulse was to present her hand to all the children seated near her so they could be witnesses to her success. She raised her eyes, her face the glowing picture of pride and elation, and her right hand poised to poke the child seated in front of her. But much to her surpise, she looked straight into the eyes of her teacher. Keeping a steady gaze that told Idalee she had observed the whole procedure, the teacher said, "Idalee, go to the board and work problem number ten."

Poor Idalee's heart sank. There was nothing to do but pick up her arithmetic book with her right hand, flex the muscles in her left hand, thus releasing the nine tiny blooms, and make her way down the aisle to the chalkboard.

As Idalee walked toward the board, the teacher gave her a knowing smile, but said nothing. She was wise enough to know that there was no need to embarrass or censor the child. The fact that Idalee could not glory in her ill-timed victory was punishment enough for being inattentive during the arithmetic lesson.

Few people are born with the knack of saying nothing or just enough at the opportune time. No repeating. No rambling from the subject at hand and including past events or future predictions. No adding of unrelated points for good measure. Just saying the right words at the right time. The rest of us must constantly strive to develop such a desired trait.

Jesus, the Master Teacher, gave us perfect examples. He spoke the right words at the right time. They needed no further explanation or elaboration. When certain of the Pharisees and Herodians attempted to ensare Jesus by asking, "Is it lawful to give tribute to Caesar, or not?" His reply was, "Render to Caesar the things that are Caesar's, and to God the things that are God's" *(Mark*

12:12-17). Who could argue with such a pithy but pointed reply?

Christ's words to the men who brought the adultress to Him were simply, "He that is without sin among you, let him first cast a stone at her." Not a single word added could have enhanced the effectiveness of His rebuke, for John tells us that "they which heard it, being convicted by their own conscience, went out one by one, beginning at the eldest, even unto the last" *(John 8:1-7).*

Jesus summed up the problems of the rich young ruler who came to Him seeking the way to inherit eternal life by saying, "It is easier for a camel to go through a needle's eye, than for a rich man to enter into the kingdom of God" *(Luke 18:18-25).*

And Mark Twain wrote this bit of wisdom:
"The difference between the right word and the almost right word is the difference between lightning and the lightning bug."

R. A. Millikan sums up all these thoughts in one terse sentence: "The things that a man does not say often reveal the understanding and penetration of his mind even more than the things he says."

Closing Hymn: My Faith Looks Up to Thee

Benediction

Dismiss us with Thy blessings, Dear Father.
May we leave this place with willing hearts filled with determination to fill our individual places, humble as they may be, to the best of our abilities each day.
May we be blessed with fellowship with the Lord, our Savior, through understanding and compassion for our fellow men. In His name we pray. Amen.

Taking Too Much for Granted

And the servant of the Lord must not strive; but be gentle unto all men, apt to teach, patient (2 Timothy 2:24).

~~~~~~

Opening Meditation

For that impatient gesture of this morning,
That unkind word which should have been suppressed,
The failure yesterday to lend a helping hand,
That selfish deed designed for personal gain,
That opportunity we failed to use
   To sympathize or try to understand,
     Most gracious Lord, forgive.
And as we seek Thy pardon, may we also
Petition for new opportunities
To serve our fellowmen through patience,
   Love, and understanding.

Opening Hymn: Make Me a Blessing

Devotional

Idalee's seventh-grade English class was reading *Silas Marner*. Certain pages were assigned each night to be retold by members of the class and discussed the following day. Idalee's assignment was that part of the story in which Silas, after being robbed of his hoarded gold, returned to his cottage one cold night and saw little Eppie asleep in front of the fire. Silas mistook Eppie's yellow curls, shining like gold in the firelight, as his stolen treasure returned to him. In relating the story, Idalee said, "Silas rushed across the room and found, not his gold, but a little child. He picked the baby up."

The teacher interrupted, saying, "He picked up the baby."

Idalee was so intent on telling the story that she missed the teacher's point. "Yes," she said, giving the teacher a puzzled look, "he picked the baby up."

"No," the teacher insisted, "he picked up the baby."

"That's what I said," Idalee repeated. "He picked the baby up."

"No," the teacher persisted. "He picked up the baby."

By that time, Idalee was so confused, she turned to the class, who looked as puzzled as she felt, and said, "Well, he did." Then she continued to relate the story without further interruptions.

22

Not until years later did Idalęe realize what her English teacher was trying to teach her that day—not to end a sentence with a preposition. The teacher was so certain Idalee would understand her correction that she did not take time to explain. She took too much for granted.

We too are often guilty of the same failing—taking too much for granted. We give incomplete instructions, expecting our children or other adults to know how we want something done. We fail to state explicitly what we expect; then when we are disappointed with their performance, we find ourselves saying, "Well, you should have known better."

Effective communication requires patience—patience in speaking plainly and simply, and patience in repeating.

The limitless patience of God manifested through the life of Christ is too awesome for us to fully comprehend. After the chosen twelve, who were closest to Christ, and His most devoted students, had heard His teachings both to the multitudes and in private, Philip said, "Lord, show us the Father, and it sufficeth us."

Christ's reply exuded the never-ending patience of a devoted teacher. "Have I been so long time with you, and yet hast thou not known me, Philip? he that hath seen me hath seen the Father; and how sayest thou then, Show us the Father?" *(John 14:8-10)*.

Whether we realize it or not, each one of us is a teacher. We not only teach through the words we speak; we teach through the examples we set. Others are influenced by what we say and do. To challenge others, especially children and young people with whom we come in contact, to do their best in whatever they attempt, we must demonstrate through our actions that we are trying to do likewise.

The German poet Goethe expressed this thought through his poem.

Best
Like the star,
That shines afar,
Without haste
And without rest,
Let each man wheel with steady sway
Round the task that rules the day,
And do his best.

In a letter dated March 11, 1887, quoted in *The Story of My Life* by Helen Keller, Annie Sullivan, the great teacher who has come to be known as "The Miracle Worker," wrote

> My heart is singing for joy this morning. A miracle has happened! The light of understanding has shone upon my little pupil's mind, and behold, all things are changed!

As we continue to study God's Word, striving for deeper knowledge, greater understanding, and an abundance of patience, may we be so blessed that we can say of our enlightenment, "A miracle has happened! The light of understanding has shone upon my mind, and behold, all things are changed!"

Closing Hymn: What a Friend We Have in Jesus

Closing Thought by E. B. Pusey:

> We have need of patience with ourselves and with others;
> with those below, and those above us, and with our own equals;
> with those who love us and those who love us not;
> for the greatest things and for the least;
> against sudden inroads of trouble, and under daily burdens;
> disappointments as to the weather, or the breaking of the heart;
> in the weariness of the body, or the wearing of the soul;
> in our own failure of duty, or others' failure toward us;
> in everyday wants, or . . . in disappointment, bereavement, losses, injuries, reproaches;
> in the heaviness of the heart, or amid delayed hopes.
> In all these things, from childhood's little troubles to the martyr's sufferings,
> patience is the grace of God whereby we endure evil for the love of God.

> May we lean heavily upon
>   the everlasting Word of God,
> From which we constantly receive
>   an outpouring of knowledge,
>   understanding, and patience,
> To strengthen our souls now and forevermore.

Expecting the Worst

How beautiful upon the mountains are the feet of him that bringeth good tidings, that publisheth peace; that bringeth good tidings of good, that publisheth salvation; that saith unto Zion, Thy God reigneth! (Isaiah 52:7).

‸‸

Opening Thought

Happiness as Defined by George Sand

One is happy as a result of one's own efforts, once one knows the necessary ingredients of happiness—simple tastes, a certain degree of courage, self-denial to a point, love of work, and, above all, a clear conscience.

Opening Hymn: He's a Wonderful Savior to Me

Devotional

The Cincinnati Choristers, a chorale of mixed voices under the direction of Ralph Hartzel, an accomplished musician and capable director, presented two formal concerts a year. To prepare for the concerts, the chorale rehearsed weekly until a month preceding the concert, when they met twice a week. The Sunday afternoon immediately preceding the concert was always reserved for the final rehearsal.

On one such occasion, the chorale assembled in the auditorium of the downtown YWCA at the appointed time, sat in their assigned seats, received their folders of music from the chorale librarian, and waited for Mr. Hartzel.

They waited fifteen minutes, twenty minutes, a half hour. No Mr. Hartzel. The longer they waited, the more apprehensive they became, for Mr. Hartzel was a perfectionist. They knew he would rehearse all afternoon and evening if necessary until he was satisfied with the performance.

Suddenly Mr. Hartzel rushed into the auditorium. "Oh, Lord, what a morning!" he shouted.

There was a dead silence. The chorale froze in their seats wondering what Mr. Hartzel was going to say and do. When he reached the podium, he picked up his baton and shouted again, more forcefully, *"Oh, Lord, what a morning!"*

The chorale sat petrified. He looked at the group and shouted a third time, "OH, LORD, WHAT A MORNING!"

No one moved.

Mr. Hartzel broke forth in jovial laughter. "Let's get the rehearsal started," he said. "Get out your music for 'Oh, Lord, What a Morning.'"

The words to that beautiful composition, "Oh, Lord, What a Morning," are a joyous expression of a jubilant soul responding to the untold wonders of God—quite a contrast to what the singers thought those same words were expressing when spoken by Mr. Hartzel as he rushed into the auditorium forty-five minutes late. They were so positive he would be aggravated and difficult to please that not one of them recognized the words as the title to one of the songs they had been rehearsing weekly for several months.

"Oh, Lord, what a morning!" may suggest disaster, chaos, unpleasantness—or it may be an expression of an exalted soul praising God for His great blessings. The way the words are spoken reflects the mood of the speaker.

We are sometimes so prone to expect disaster that we see and hear everything in that light. We expect disaster, so we look for disaster. We expect trouble, so we look for trouble. We expect disappointment, so we look for disappointment. We are so certain an experience will be an unpleasant one, we bend all efforts (consciously or otherwise) to have our expectations fulfilled.

Someone said it like this: "Pessimists have good appetites." We might add, "And they thrive on chaos, adversities, and calamities."

On one occasion when Jesus sent His disciples into a nearby town to buy food, He lingered beside the well in the city in Samaria near the parcel of land that Jacob had given to Joseph. A woman approached the well, earthen jug in hand, to draw a supply of water. She recognized Jesus as a Jew, and therefore expected no exchange of words, since deep-rooted hatred had existed between the two nations for centuries.

But in the presence of Jesus, all things are possible. All of the woman's sins were known to Him, but instead of condemning her, He offered her a drink, not just of water from the well to refresh her body, but of living water to save her soul *(John 4:3-15)*.

Robert Southey, Poet Laureate of England (1813) left us these thoughts on minimizing our troubles and disappointments and maximizing our blessings:

I have told you of the man who always put on his spectacles when about to eat cherries, in order that the fruit might look larger and more tempting. In like manner I always make the most of my enjoyments, and, though I do not cast my eyes away from troubles, I pack them into as small a compass as I can for myself, and never let them annoy others.

Closing Hymn: My Redeemer

Closing Thought by the poet, Sara Teasdale

> Joy is a flame in me
>   Too steady to destroy.

Obedience, God's First Law

And being found in fashion as a man, he humbled himself, and became obedient unto death, even the death of the cross (Philippians 2:8).

~~~~~~

Opening Meditation

Oh Christ, our Lord of life through death,
And of love, through overcoming hate,
We worship Thee in holiness
Of beauty and submissive will.
May troubled souls and fearful hearts
Find peace and faith renewed in Thee
    through obedience.
May we, though feeble when apart
From Thee, find our courage and our strength
Restored through our obedience
Unto Thy Word and unto Thy way of life.

Opening Hymn: Trust and Obey

Devotional

The new first-grade teacher wanted to train her children to leave the classroom at the end of each school day as tidy as possible and in an orderly fashion. So at the end of the second day, the teacher told the children they were going to play a game to see who could put their chairs under the tables more quietly—the girls or the boys. The teacher explained that she would turn around with her back to the children, close her eyes, and say, "Girls." The girls would then put their chairs as quietly as possible under the table. When she said, "Boys," the boys would do likewise. She would listen carefully and decide which group won.

The children thought this would be great fun, so the contest began. When the teacher turned her back and said, "Girls," there was practically no sound in the room, but the teacher sensed that something more than merely pushing chairs under the tables was taking place. There was the same kind of awareness when it was the boys' turn.

When the teacher turned around, amid complete silence, not a chair was visible. The children had done exactly what she had told them to do. They had turned their chairs backs down and placed them on the floor, under the tables. A remarkable accomplishment for first graders without making the slightest sound! And a valuable lesson in obedience!

Would that we brought such a childish sense of obedience to every situation in our lives. Would that we had such a desire to please God by bending every effort to comply with His Word and His laws to the nth degree.

Michel Montaigne, French essayist of the sixteenth century, thus expressed his strong conviction that obedience is the essence of the relationship between man and God:

> The first law that ever God gave to man was a law of obedience; it was a commandment pure and simple, wherein man had nothing to inquire after or to dispute, for as much as to obey is the proper office of a rational soul acknowledging a heavenly superior and benefactor. . . . From obedience and submission spring all other virtues, as all sin does from self-opinion and self-will.

The Scriptures gives us many examples of the rewards of obedience and the punishments because of disobedience. The first example is the expulsion of Adam and Eve from the Garden of Eden because they disregarded God's command *(Genesis 3)*.

Another classic example of the latter is Lot's wife, who, having received the special blessing of being saved from the brimstone and fire destruction of Sodom and Gomorrah, disobeyed God's command, looked back, and became a pillar of salt *(Genesis 19:1-26)*.

On the opposite end of the spectrum, we find Abraham was obedient to God's command even to stretching forth his hand and taking the knife to slay Isaac, his son, upon the altar *(Genesis 22:1-13)*.

Joseph, the humble carpenter of Nazareth, exemplified unwavering devotion to God through his complete obedience to God's commands, first to marry Mary, about to become the mother of the Christ, God's Son; and later, when the angel of the Lord appeared to Joseph in a dream, saying, "Arise, and take the young child and his mother, and flee into Egypt, and be thou there until I bring thee word: for Herod will seek the young child to destroy him" *(Matthew 2:13)*, Joseph obeyed without question, doubt, or hesitation.

As the Son of God, Jesus commanded the same obedience of all who would follow after Him, for He, himself, was obedient to the command and the will of God even to His death on Calvary.

"Go, wash in the pool of Siloam," Jesus instructed the blind man.

And we read that "He went his way therefore, and washed, and came seeing" *(John 9:1-7)*.

"How will you find good?" George Eliot asked. "It is not a thing of choice; it is a river that flows from the foot of the invisible throne, and flows by the path of obedience."

Thomas Watson, an English clergyman of the seventeenth century, expressed these thoughts in a simple way:

To obey God in some things, and not in others, shows an unsound heart. Childlike obedience moves toward every command of God as the needle points where the loadstone draws.

A loadstone (also lodestone) is a magnetized piece of ore used by sailors to guide their course. What an apropos concluding thought—a relationship between obedience to God and a well-charted useful life.

Closing Hymn: Have Thine Own Way, Lord

Closing Thought

Obedience

To find God we must return
To the first law that He gave man—
The law demanding our obedience.
There is no choice for us to make.
A law so clearly defined should
Avoid dispute or questioning.
Obedience demands complete submission.
Doing what God wills, not what we will,
Leaves little time for doubting His plans.
Obedience not only leads us to God;
From it spring all virtues
And God's promises fulfilled.

Encouraging Individuality

Let your light so shine before men, that they may see your good works, and glorify your Father which is in heaven (Matthew 5:16).

~~~~~~

Opening Meditation

How great are Thy works, O God.
How beautiful are Thy creations.
We bow in awesome wonder as we see
Thy works in the brilliant autumn sunsets—
In the snow-filled winter skies—
In the resurrected life of spring—
In the radiant galaxies of a summer night—
In the reverent silence of sun-baked deserts—
In the lofty towering mountain peaks.
But even more wonderful than all of these
Are the unique differences
Thou hast created in each one of us.
May we treasure these precious gifts of individuality.
May we conscientiously strive to develop to the highest potential
Each of our original, God-given talents, traits, and personalities.

Opening Hymn: Follow the Gleam

Devotional

The Publicity Director of a church-affiliated children's home was filling the vacant position of housemother to sixteen high-school girls. As such, she spent her days in the office and her nights with the girls.

After school one day, a girl came to the office and asked her housemother to remind her to take along a bag of soil the next morning for her horticulture class. Just before bedtime, the housemother remembered the bag of soil but had forgotten which girl needed it, as several had popped into the office after school that day making similar requests. So she interrupted the study hour.

"Who asked me to remind you to take a bag of soil to school tomorrow?" she asked.

Before anyone could reply, one girl giggled and said, "You mean a sack of ground."

Immediately another girl said, "You mean a toot of dirt."

And promptly a third girl said, "You mean a poke of earth."

The four girls came from four different states. Each had her individual way of expression, and while the words varied, the meaning was the same.

Just as different words can express the same thought, so there are different ways of doing a given task, different ways of accomplishing the same goal. And these different ways reflect the individuality of each of us.

It is sometimes difficult to accept personality differences, especially in our homes. We recognize that no two individuals are identical even though members of the same family. Yet too often we seem unable to make allowances for ideas, actions, or interests that differ from our own.

Of individuality Emerson wrote,

> Every individual nature has its own beauty. In every company, at every fireside, one is struck with the riches of nature, when he hears so many tones, all musical, sees in each person original manners which have a proper and peculiar charm, and reads new expressions of face. He perceives that nature had laid for each the foundations of a divine building if the soul will build thereon.

Perhaps there is no more illustrious example of the importance of individuality to the success of a life than Edward W. Bok, who, through developing original ideas and pursuing imaginative methods, rose from a poor boy of Dutch immigrant parents to the editor of *Ladies' Home Journal,* leaving as a fitting memorial the beautiful Bok Bell Tower in Florida. He believed that "The present is the time of all times for the individual man: the individual will: the individual mind: the individual energy."

The greatest example of individuality is Jesus Christ. William Day Simonds presents an inspiring picture of Christ as an individual whose will was to conform with no tenet or law or practice that was contrary to the Word of His Heavenly Father.

Jesus was the incarnation of the Spirit that allays strife, changes animosity to friendship—His was the spirit that helps and heals.

Jesus was the Prince of Peace as between man and man, nation and nation, race and race.

Jesus was the Prince of Compassion. He saw the multitude poor and distressed and said, with infinite tenderness, "I have compassion on the multitude."

Jesus was the Prince of Forgiveness and taught the deadliness of hate to the one who hates.

Jesus was the Prince of Love. His royal proclamation was "Come unto me, and I will give you rest."

His last benediction was, "Peace I leave with you, my peace I give unto you."

Closing Hymn: The Touch of His Hand on Mine

Closing Thought

Dismiss us with Thy blessing, dear Father.
May we part one from another with the willingness of heart to fill our
individual places, humble or important as they may be,
To the best of our abilities.
May we be blessed with fellowship with our Lord and Savior
Through expressions of loving kindness to our fellowmen.
In the name of Christ we pray. Amen.

The Sign of Greatness

Humble yourselves therefore under the mighty hand of God, that he may exalt you in due time (1 Peter 5:6).

~~~~~~

Opening Meditation

> Prayer is like the wings of the eagle;
> It carries us above the cares of this world
> To heights that otherwise are unknown to man.
> Prayer is like a desert oasis;
> It refreshes and nourishes the barren soul.
> Prayer is like the radiance of dawn;
> It brings hope for new light to darkened life.
> Prayer humbles even the greatest among us,
> For when we are in prayer
> We are in the presence of Almighty God,
> Creator and Ruler of the universe.

Opening Hymn: Sweet Hour of Prayer

Devotional

Two farm ladies were discussing the relative merits of their preachers.

"And how do you like your new minister?" one of them asked.

"Well," the other lady began, "I'm not one to go all out for anything right off. Not like most of the congregation. I take my time and look things over before I decide. Oh, he can preach a good sermon. How that man can preach! And when it comes to knowing the Bible, why he can quote Scripture by the hour. And pray! I never heard a preacher who could pray like him. And when it comes to ministering to the sick, that man's as gentle as a woman and a pillar of strength. But, as I said, I'm not one to make up my mind right off. So whenever anybody asked me, 'How do you like our new preacher?' I just said, 'I'll tell you after butcherin.'

"Well, it just happened that it was our turn to butcher first this year. That morning when we got up, I said to Ezra, 'Ezra, before this day is over, I'll tell you how I like our new preacher.' I watched from the kitchen window. The preacher arrived in the first carload. He was dressed just like the other men—overalls and knee boots (brand new). I watched him all day. That man was as handy as the pocket on a shirt. That night I said to Ezra, 'Ezra, we are surely blessed. We've got a great preacher.'"

What a great preacher that man must have been! With all the described noble attributes he possessed, he still was humble enough to be part of a community project which was not only completely out of his field, but none too pleasant at best.

True greatness might be defined as achieving outstanding recognition in a chosen field but still being humble enough to step out of an important role, or step down from an important position, to perform a menial task—and perform it willingly and well. False pride is often used as veneering to conceal an insecure person. When someone feels himself too good or too important to do a job he considers beneath his dignity or station, he broadcasts to those about him that not only is he aware of his deficiencies; he also senses insecurity.

Dwight L. Moody left us a pithy but wise adage: "Be humble or you'll stumble."

J. R. Lowell wrote, "Humbleness is always grace, always dignity."

Emerson commented, "It is the mark of nobleness to volunteer the lowest service, the greatest spirit only attaining to humility."

Phillips Brooks left us this challenging thought: "The true way to be humble is not to stoop till you are smaller than yourself, but to stand at your real height against some higher nature that shall show you what the real smallness of your greatness is."

When the disciples came to Jesus asking, "Who is the greatest in the kingdom of heaven?" Jesus called a little child unto Him, and set him in the midst of them.

"Verily I say unto you," Jesus told them, "Except ye be converted, and become as little children, ye shall not enter into the kingdom of heaven. Whosoever therefore shall humble himself as this little child, the same is greatest in the kingdom of heaven" *(Matthew 18:1-4)*.

When Christ's earthly life was nearing the end, He gave us an example of humility by washing the feet of His disciples *(John 13:1-17)*.

Closing Hymn: O, for a Closer Walk With God

Closing Thought

Charles Reade, one of England's outstanding nineteenth century novelists, observed,

Not a day passes over the earth but men and women of no note do great deeds, speak great words, and suffer noble sorrows. Of these obscure heroes, philosophers, and martyrs the greater part will never be known till that hour when many that were great shall be small and the small shall be great.

Too Much Too Soon?

Blessed is that steward, whom his lord when he cometh shall find so doing (Luke 12:43).

~~~~~~

Opening Meditation

Stewardship means taking maximum care
Of every gift that God has entrusted to our use.
We mortals have long abused the use of *my* and *mine*—
My house. *My* car. *My* money. That or this is *mine*.
In reality, all things have been created by God,
Loaned to us for a brief and fleeting span of time,
To be recalled by the Great Giver of all things,
At any moment.
Let us not be found unworthy stewards,
Traitors to the trust God has placed in us;
Rather let us be worthy of His never-ending love and generosity
By using with wisdom and frugality
God's natural and material gifts to us.

Opening Hymn: This Is My Father's World

Devotional

One of the delights of working with young children is to observe them at a celebration. They particularly love birthday parties. Even two- and three-year olds will sit quietly on their miniature chairs, eagerly awaiting the exciting moment when the candles on the birthday cake will be lit. As soon as the first candle begins to flicker, they begin to chant happily, "Happy birthday to you! Happy birthday to you!"

Seeing the cake in the middle of the table, watching the candles glow, and enjoying the cake with their friends is complete happiness.

Most of us give our children too much too soon. We are so anxious to provide material things that we frequently thwart, even destroy, their appreciation for the truly delightful moments of life. They may become incapable of appreciating even expensive gifts or unusual experiences.

A first grader opened a new box of forty-eight assorted crayons, broke the first three that she used, then tossed the entire box into the wastebasket. Her teacher, who had observed the waste, questioned the child as to why she threw the crayons away.

"I don't like to use broken crayons," she explained. "My mother will buy me another box. We go to the supermarket every day, and she buys whatever I put in the shopping cart."

A third-grade boy had a new five-hundred-sheet pack of notebook paper in his desk. He drew a careless doodle in the middle of a sheet, cumpled it into a ball, and tossed it in the direction of the wastebasket. He repeated the procedure six times in rapid succession before his teacher questioned him.

"Oh, that's all right," he replied. "I have four more packages at home."

At another school, the teachers were operating on a close budget which necessitated handling all supplies, including paper toweling, in a frugal manner in order to stretch them the entire semester. Each teacher was given an allotment of paper toweling for her class, and she doled out the daily supply to each child as he washed his hands before lunch. About the fourth day of school one of the first graders came armed with a giant roll of paper toweling along with a note from her mother which read, "Mrs. Vonk, this roll of toweling is for Susan's use only. She uses as many paper towels as she likes when she washes her hands at home. When this roll is used, I'll send another."

Every teacher has found herself wondering on similar occasions whatever happened to the time-worn maxim, "Waste not, want not."

Encouraging children to acquire an extravagant taste for material things is to handicap them. Young people who are given all they demand (and more) as children are deprived of the ability to find joy and appreciation in the little but beautiful things in life, and this characteristic is carried over into adult life as well. Furthermore, in this day of ecological heralding, when and where should conservation and appreciation begin?

Gifford Pinchot, a pioneer in planning conservation of the nation's forests, defined conservation as "the wise use of the earth and its resources for the lasting good of man." Surely "the wise use of the earth and its resources" must include children, for we are creatures of habit, and habits are formed when we are children.

One of Benjamin Franklin's many wise axioms warns, "It is easier to suppress the first desire than to satisfy all that follow it."

The foundation for good stewardship must be laid in the home through teaching and through example, for as George Horne, English bishop of the 18th century, explained:

Our children, relations, friends, honors, houses, lands, and endowments, the goods of nature and fortune, nay, even of grace itself, are only lent. It is our misfortune, and our sin, to fancy they are given. We start, therefore, and are angry when the loan is called in. We think of ourselves masters, when we are only stewards, and forget that to each of us it will one day be said, "Give an account of thy stewardship."

Adolph Monod, a Swiss clergyman and contemporary of Horne expressed the same sentiments:

There is no portion of our time that is our time, and the rest God's; there is no portion of money that is our money, and the rest God's money. It is all His; He made it all, gives it all, and He has simply trusted it to us for His service. A servant has two purses, the master's and his own, but we have only one.

Let a man so account of us, as of the ministers of Christ, and stewards of the mysteries of God *(1 Corinthians 4:1)*.

Closing Hymn: The Lord Is My Shepherd

Closing Thought

As our parting thoughts on stewardship, let us combine the words of Charles Simmons, an American clergyman, with those of George Horne and Adolph Monod.

As to all that we have and are, we are but stewards of the most high God. On all our possessions, on our time, and talents, and influence, and property, He has written, "Occupy for me, and till I shall come." To obey His instructions and serve Him faithfully is the true test of obedience and discipleship.

Transforming Clouds Into Pigs

And how shall they preach, except they be sent? as it is written, How beautiful are the feet of them that preach the gospel of peace, and bring glad tidings of good things! (Romans 10:15).

vvvvvvvvvvvvvvvvvvvvvvvvvvvvvvvvvvvvvvvvvvvvvvvvvvvvv

Opening Meditation

Emily Dickinson wrote,
>A word is dead
>When it is said,
>Some say.
>I say it just
>Begins to live
>That day.

If only words that are happy, joyous, encouraging, comforting, and full of praise and adoration lived on,

Our world would be transformed in many ways.

But unfortunately words of criticism, rejection, hatred, jealousy, and prejudice do not die as soon as they are spoken.

Therefore, since we have been given mastery over our speech,

And since we have the patience and understanding of Jesus as our life's model,

What we say, how we say it, when and why the words were spoken

Should be of great concern to us each time we open our mouths and permit even just one word to pass our lips.

Opening Hymn: Beautiful Words of Jesus

Devotional

An editor had a large, framed black and white etching hanging over her desk. For more than two years she enjoyed the picture every time her eyes rested upon it. The theme was a beautiful landscape, a quiet, restful pastoral scene. There were gently rolling hills, silhouetted trees, some gracefully symmetrical, some gnarled, some windswept, but all adding beauty to the countryside. The sky was a mass of billowy clouds which, though all black and white, suggested joys of a balmy day in early spring, alive with all the rich odors of the good earth.

40

Then one day a writer brought in copy for his regular column. He passed the editor's desk and, as usual, stopped to chat. On this occasion, he glanced up at the etching and remarked. "I'm surprised you'd have a picture of a pig over your desk."

"A pig!" the editor echoed, wondering what he was talking about.

Then, taking an eighteen-inch ruler, the writer leaned over the desk and in the cloud formation outlined what the editor had to admit was a perfect pig—curling tail, snout, and all.

From that moment, each time the editor looked at the picture, all she could see was the big pig. Before the week was over, she had requested the custodian to remove the picture.

Some people go through life changing clouds into pigs. They are not satisfied to keep their skepticism, doubts, suspicions, or dissatisfaction to themselves. They feel compelled to relay them to family, friends, acquaintances, or anyone who happens by. They ignore the beautiful, and have eyes only for what they consider the imperfect. They take pleasure in going out of their way to transform beauty into ugliness. And having done so, they seem to derive personal satisfaction from the shock or dismay they have created. But he who delights in transforming clouds into pigs not only destroys present joys and spreads discontent; he robs himself of the great beauties of life and the real joy of living.

In contrast, consider the message of this letter received by a Children's Home, along with a sizeable check representing money a Sunday-school class of ten-year-old boys had raised as a result of Timmy.

"Timmy's soul is as straight as his spine is crooked," his Sunday-school teacher wrote. "Already he has suffered greater pain during his ten years on this earth than most adults suffer their entire life. But what an inspiration he is to all of us! He sees only the beautiful. He thinks only the good. He speaks only love and inspiration. His twisted little body houses a heart so big everyone who knows him feels compelled to become a better Christian."

Theodosia Garrison, an American poet, described a friend who was quite unlike the writer who transformed clouds into pigs, but a kindred spirit to little Timmy:

I never crossed your threshold with a grief
But that I went away without it.

Through His parables and His miracles, Christ exemplified a life committed to alleviating pain, not to increasing it; to eradicating unkindness, not to perpetuating it; to removing misunderstandings, not to kindling them; to transforming hatred into love.

"My peace I leave with you," Christ promised. But each of us must be a willing and worthy recipient of that great blessing.

Closing Hymn: Abide With Me

Closing Thought

By cultivating the beautiful, we scatter the seeds of heavenly flowers, as by doing good we cultivate those that belong to humanity.

—John Howard.

Not All Bargains Are Bargains

And Jesus said, Somebody hath touched me: for I perceive that virtue is gone out of me (Luke 8:46).

~~~~~~

Opening Meditation

Let us remember our Lord and Savior, Jesus Christ, who revealed to us an exalted example of self-dedication when He said,

"Verily, verily, I say unto you, I am the door of the sheep.

All that ever came before me are thieves and robbers: but the sheep did not hear them.

I am the door: by me if any man enter in, he shall be saved, and shall go in and out, and find pasture.

The thief cometh not, but for to steal, and to kill, and to destroy: I am come that they might have life, and that they might have it more abundantly.

I am the good shepherd: the good shepherd giveth his life for his sheep.

Therefore doth my Father love me, because I lay down my life, that I might take it again.

No man taketh it from me, but I lay it down of myself.

I have power to lay it down, and I have power to take it again.

This commandment have I received of my Father"

<div align="right">(John 10:7-11, 17, 18).</div>

Opening Hymn: I Gave My Life for Thee

Devotional

During World War II, a small department store was having its annual clearance sale of surplus open-stock china. A regular customer came into the store, saw the sign, *Saucers 1¢ Each,* and asked, "Is that right? Are those saucers really just one cent each, or did you mean ten cents each?"

When the manager assured him the sign was correct, he said, "That's the biggest bargain I've ever seen. Saucers one cent each! I'll take a dozen."

After carrying his purchase to his car, he came back and bought ten more saucers.

That afternoon, he brought his wife with him to select wallpaper for the room they were redecorating. Before looking at the samples, he ushered her to the gift department, showed her the saucers, and said, "See! Saucers for one cent each! Just like I told you!"

They selected their wallpaper, but before leaving, he again guided his wife to the gift department and said, "Don't you think we should buy more saucers?"

His wife gave him a patient smile and said, "Honey, we don't need more saucers."

"But it's such a bargain," he insisted. "Saucers one cent each!"

"But we have enough saucers," she said patiently.

"But just *one cent each!*"

At this point, still smiling at him patiently, she said in a kind but firm voice, "Honey, we don't use saucers!"

They did not purchase more saucers then, but just before closing time that evening, the man rushed in and asked, "Have you sold all of those saucers?"

"No," the manager said. "I think there are ten or twelve left."

"I'll take all of them," he said. "I'll never find such a bargain again."

True, a saucer for a penny is a bargain, but only if you have need for it. Perhaps Kin Hubbard had individuals like this man in mind when he wrote, "It makes no difference what it is, some people will buy anything they think a store is losing money on."

Unfortunately, some people assume a bargain-hunting attitude toward religion. They might agree with James Mason: "It will cost something to be religious, but it will cost more not to be." Still, they are unwilling to pay the high price demanded of them. They never permit their roots to grow deeply into the fertile soil of any one church in order to avoid assuming any financial or personal obligation to support the work of a particular congregation.

"Creeds grow so thick along the way their boughs hide God," Lizette Woodworth Reese warned, "but many restless individuals flitter from one man-made creed to another, trying to find what can only be found by the true follower of Christ."

There is no such being as a bargain Christian. How can there be? The price of Christianity was costly and was paid in full by Jesus Christ. As Martin Luther reminds us, "In his life, Christ is an example, showing us how to live; in his death, he is a sacrifice, satisfying for our sins; in his resurrection, a conqueror; in his ascension, a king; in his intercession, a high priest."

"Christianity works while infidelity talks," Henry Ward Beecher

44

wrote. "She feeds the hungry, clothes the naked, visits and cheers the sick, and seeks the lost, while infidelity abuses her and babbles nonsense and profanity. 'By their fruits ye shall know them.' "

The Christian life is not merely hearing the Word of God, studying the Word of God, and knowing the Word of God. The Christian life is doing the will of Christ so that others may see Him in all phases of your life.

Closing Hymn: O, Jesus, I Have Promised

Closing Thought

Self-dedication is contagious. Many great Christian movements for humanity's good have developed out of the self-dedication of a single individual.

A Little Bending, A Little Stretching

And besides this, giving all diligence, add to your faith virtue; and to virtue, knowledge; and to knowledge, temperance; and to temperance, patience; and to patience, godliness; and to godliness, brotherly kindness; and to brotherly kindness, charity (2 Peter 1:5-7).

~~~~~~

Opening Meditation

Kindness Is Never Lost

Like every other virtue,
Kindness is twice blessed;
It leaves a blessing with the one
Who sends a kindness on its way,
And also blesses the recipient.
Kind acts reveal our souls.
Kind words are like mirrors
Which reflect our minds
And show what we hold secret
In our hearts. A kindness
Then, conferred, is never lost.

Opening Hymn: My Prayer (More Holiness Give Me)

Devotional

One afternoon a husband and wife came into a store, arguing. Apparently, they had been quarreling for some time to be in such a heated controversy. It made no difference to them that other customers were present. They made no attempt to lower their voices or halt their exchange of biting words.

The dispute concerned the decorating materials they had come to purchase. The woman was determined that the room would be decorated in one color scheme, and the man was just as determined that it would be another. They stood in different aisles with stacks of paint cans between them, and the poor clerk stood at the end of the aisle, feeling much like a referee at a wrestling match.

In time the man asked for a yardstick to help him ascertain a measurement. The clerk went behind the counter, picked up a yardstick, and handed it to the woman, who stood nearer the counter. The woman extended her arm stiffly to hand the yardstick over the wall of paint cans to her husband. He, in turn, extended his arm stiffly to receive it, but there were about four inches between the end of the yardstick and his hand. If either had leaned slightly forward—not taking a step, just bending slightly—the yardstick would have easily reached his hand. But neither would give the other even so small a degree of simple courtesy.

Instead, they stood glaring at each other as if to insist it was the responsibility of the other to make the effort. The clerk walked from behind the counter, took the yardstick from the woman's hand, closed the four-inch gap, and gave it to the man.

Bitterness is closely akin to hatred. It can destroy a personality, change an individual's goals or purpose in life, and deprive a person of self-respect.

To establish and maintain a wholesome relationship, there must be some stretching and bending on the part of each individual. The closer the relationship, the more stretching and bending is necessary; but the closer the relationship, the easier it should be to give that added measure of consideration, that special kind of understanding, that respect for the wishes and ideas of each other.

We teach our children Julia Carney's song about doing deeds of kindness. As adults, we would benefit from thinking about the words of that meaningful verse:

Little deeds of kindness, little words of love,

Help to make earth happy, like the heaven above.

On one occasion when Jesus had astonished the multitude with His teachings, one of the listening Pharisees asked Him a question, tempting Him to make a response contrary to their doctrines. "Master, which is the great commandment in the law?" he asked.

Jesus answered, "Thou shalt love the Lord thy God with all thy heart, and with all thy soul, and with all thy mind. This is the first and great commandment. And the second is like unto it, Thou shalt love thy neighbour as thyself. On these two commandments hang all the law and the prophets" (Matthew 22:33-40).

The first great commandment expresses what our relationship with God should be as covered by the first four Commandments; the second commandment expresses what our relationship with others should be as covered by the last six Commandments (Exodus 20:1-17).

There are days when the world seems rushing by so fast we can hardly keep pace with it, let alone take time for acts of neighborly love. But regardless of how crowded one's daily schedule might become, there's little excuse for failing to speak a kind word, even to a stranger.

In her homey style, Carrie Jacobs Bond reminds us,

Kind words smooth all the "Paths o' Life"
And smiles make burdens light.
And uncomplainin' friends can make
A daytime out o' night.

Closing Hymn: Trusting Jesus

Closing Thought

When Eleanor H. Porter wrote *Pollyanna* in 1912, she had no way of knowing that seventy years later her heroine would still be regarded as the epitome of the power and influence kind words have over all who hear them.

What men and women need is encouragement. Their natural resisting powers should be strengthened, not weakened. . . . Instead of always harping on a man's faults, tell him of his virtues. Try to pull him out of his rut of bad habits. Hold up to him his better self, his *real* self that can dare and do and win out! . . . The influence of a beautiful, helpful, hopeful character is contagious, and many revolutionize a whole town. . . . People radiate what is in their minds and in their hearts. If a man feels kindly and obliging, his neighbors will feel that way, too, before long. But if he scolds and scowls and criticizes—his neighbors will return scowl for scowl, and add interest! (from Chapter 22 of *Pollyanna)*

Making Decisions

Now faith is the substance of things hoped for, the evidence of things not seen (Hebrews 11:1).

~~~~~~

Opening Meditation

From the Psalms
When I consider the heavens, the work of thy fingers,
The moon and the stars, which thou hast ordained;
What is man, that thou art mindful of him?
And the son of man, that thou visitest him?
Thou coverest thyself with light as with a garment.
Thou stretchest out the heavens like a curtain.
Thou makest the clouds thy chariot.
Thou walkest upon the wings of the wind.
   Let us worship the God who reigned then,
   Reigns now,
   And shall reign forever more.

Opening Hymn: My Faith Looks Up to Thee

Devotional

A mother, a nine-year-old daughter, and a four-year-old son were Christmas shopping. The little boy decided he wanted to purchase a tie for his dad's Christmas gift, but he couldn't decide which one he liked best. In time he narrowed his choice down to two. But the important question still remained: which one of those two ties should he choose?

The saleslady was most understanding and very patient. The boy had saved his own money for the gift, and the mother did not want to sway his choice. Also, she felt this was an opportunity for him to learn to make a decision.

Finally the boy looked up at his mother and said, "I can't decide which to choose. I'll have to count out." So he began aloud, pointing at each tie in turn, "Eeny, meeny, miney, mo. Catch the birdie by the toe. If he sings, then let him go. Eeny, meeny—" He stopped abruptly. "Oh, oh!" he said. "It's coming out wrong!"

Isn't that the way we sometimes arrive at a decision? First we seek the counsel of others, convinced that we have an open mind. Then

49

we move to other means of deciding when we subconsciously reject the advice given us by friends, because their advice is contrary to what our subconscious has already decided.

Being unable to make a decision sometimes reflects a pattern of procrastination that has developed in many areas of our lives. Don Marquis wrote, "Procrastination is the art of keeping up with yesterday." Procrastination also is an ever-increasing obstacle, hindering our progress and retarding our personal and spiritual growth.

We recognize the wisdom as well as the warning in the words of C. H. Lorimer, "Putting off an easy thing makes it hard, and putting off a hard one makes it impossible."

Elbert Hubbard, the American sage who lost his life on the Lusitania, observed, "It does not take much strength to do things, but it requires great strength to decide what to do."

One of the most common causes of procrastination is the inability to make a decision. Many who have not accepted Christ as their Savior have been on the brink of doing so for years—some all their lives. They, like Agrippa, are almost persuaded to be a Christian (Acts 26:28). Almost ready to make the all-important decision of their lives, but lacking sufficient faith in God's promises and everlasting care to place their lives completely in His hands and live by faith.

Some who have accepted Christ have never made the full commitment to place all phases of their lives in His care. They, to a lesser degree, have not completely accepted the fact that for every decision we must make, God has provided us with specific guidelines through the Scriptures.

The greatest deterring factor in the failure of some to accept Christ and in others to make a total commitment is the lack of faith that God knows what is best for us; that God will provide what is best for us when the right time comes for us to receive such blessings; and that everything works for good for those who love the Lord.

One day the disciples said to Jesus, "Increase our faith." And the Lord said, "If ye had faith as a grain of mustard seed, ye might say unto this sycamine tree, Be thou plucked up by the root, and be thou planted in the sea; and it should obey you" (Luke 17:5, 6).

On another occasion after Christ had cast out the devil from an afflicted child, the disciples asked, "Why could not we cast him out?" Jesus told them, "Because of your unbelief: for verily I say unto you, If ye have faith as a grain of mustard seed, ye shall say unto this mountain, Remove hence to yonder place; and it shall remove: and nothing shall be impossible unto you" (Matthew 17:19, 20).

Carved in Arabic over the main entrance arch to Granada, Spain, are these words of an ancient poet:

Give him alms, woman,
for there is nothing in life,
nothing,
so sad as to be blind in Granada.

We might paraphrase that idea and say, "Give him faith, people, for there is nothing in life, nothing, so sad as to be blind to the great love and tender mercies of God, which are ours in accordance to our measure of faith."

Closing Hymn: Almost Persuaded

Closing Thought

"Faith makes all evil good to us, and all good better; unbelief makes all good evil, and all evil worse. Faith laughs at the shaking of the spear; unbelief trembles at the shaking of a leaf. Unbelief starves the soul; faith finds food in famine, and a table in the wilderness. In the greatest danger, faith says, 'I have a great God.' When outward strength is broken, faith rests on promises. In the midst of sorrow, faith draws the string out of every trouble, and takes the bitterness from every affliction."

These words by Richard Cecil, an English clergyman, only begin to describe the great blessings awaiting us according to our faith.

The Short End of a Bargain

Grace be with all them that love our Lord Jesus Christ in sincerity (Ephesians 6:24).

〜〜〜〜〜〜〜〜〜〜〜〜〜〜〜〜〜〜〜〜〜〜〜〜〜〜

Opening Meditation

Sincerity

Sincerity—to say the things we mean
And mean the things we say;
To stand upon the truth with firm conviction
Despite harsh criticism or disloyal friends.
Sincerity—to be the things we claim to be
Without defrauding others or ourselves;
To keep each promise that we make
With punctuality and willingness.
Sincerity—to act and speak the way
We would have others act and speak to us.
Sincerity means rising from deceit
To upright ways of honesty and truth.

Opening Hymn: More Like the Master

Devotional

One hot, sultry day in Miami, Mrs. Vonk prepared ice tea for herself, expecting to serve three-and-a-half-year-old Claire her usual glass of milk with her lunch. When Claire saw her mother's glass of ice tea, she informed her in her usual positive way, that she, too, would enjoy a glass of ice tea. So Mrs. Vonk prepared a mixture for her—ice water with just enough tea added to give it a slight color.

Claire looked at the two glasses and promptly asked, "Mommy, why is your ice tea so much darker than mine?"

"Well," Mrs. Vonk began to hedge, "you see, tea, and even milk looks different in different glasses. Some glasses make whatever you pour into them look darker than they look in other glasses." This, of course, was true even though she was making the unrelated point to evade the real issue. In fact, to deceive her daughter.

"Well," Claire said, exchanging the glasses, "if there's no difference, then you drink my tea and I'll drink yours 'cause I like the darker color."

To save face, Mrs. Vonk sipped a glass of faintly colored ice water while her three-and-a-half-year-old daughter told her several times during lunch how delicious the dark colored tea was. Mrs. Vonk got the short end of a bargain she really deserved. While she told the truth in reply to her daughter's question, she had attempted to deceive; and her deception backfired.

Isn't this the way deception usually works? We attempt to conceal the truth, to sidestep the truth, to divert attention from the truth, hoping to sway the situation according to our wishes or plans for our own personal benefits. When deception backfires, as it frequently does, we find ourselves forced to accept the consequences, as unpleasant as they usually are, as the end result of the self-imposed short end of a bargain.

William Cullen Bryant expressed his feelings concerning deception rather forcefully: "Hateful to me, as are the gates of hell, is he who, hiding one thing in his heart, utters another."

O, what a tanged web we weave,
When first we practice to deceive.

These words of Walter Scott are just as true today as they were when he penned them over a hundred years ago.

Oliver Wendell Holmes gives us a more recent thought: "Sin has many tools, but a lie is the handle that fits them all."

We seldom deceive for a good purpose, and the ill fruits of our deception generally are harvested by ourselves. John Everton, an American clergyman, reminds us that "To speak or act a lie is alike contemptible in the sight of God and man."

A man named Ananias with his wife Sapphira sold a piece of property, kept back some of the proceeds, and brought only a part and laid it at the apostles' feet. But Peter said, "Ananias, why has Satan filled your heart to lie to the Holy Spirit and to keep back part of the proceeds of the land? While it remained unsold, did it not remain your own? And after it was sold, was it not at your disposal? How is it that you have contrived this deed in your heart? You have not lied to men but to God."

When Ananias heard these words, he fell down and died. And great fear came upon all who heard of it (Acts 5:1-15 RSV).

Who shall ascend into the hill of the Lord?
Or who shall stand in his holy place?
He that hath clean hands, and a pure heart;
who hath not lifted up his soul unto vanity,
nor sworn deceitfully.

He shall receive the blessing from the Lord,
and righteousness from the God of his salvation.

(Psalm 24:3-5)

Closing Hymn: I Need Thee Every Hour

Closing Thought

In his work, "The Grandmother," Alfred Lord Tennyson had this to say about deception through lying:

A lie which is half a truth is
ever the blackest of lies:
A lie which is all a lie may be
met and fought outright—
But a lie which is part a truth is a
harder matter to fight.

May the words of our mouths and the meditation of our hearts be acceptable to Thee, our God and our Creator.

Showing Compassion

Rejoice with them that do rejoice, and weep with them that weep (Romans 12:15).

~~~~~~

Opening Meditation

Except the Lord conduct the plan,
The best concerted schemes are vain,
    And never can succeed;
We spend our wretched strength for naught;
But if our works in Thee be wrought,
    They shall be blest indeed.

These words are one stanza of a poem by Charles Wesley. His brother, John, in his *Rules of Conduct,* left us a challenge for our everyday living:

Do all the good you can,
In all the ways you can,
In all the places you can,
At all the times you can,
To all the people you can,
As long as ever you can.

Opening Hymn: Lead On, O King Eternal

Devotional

A teacher's parents passed away within twenty-three days of each other. When her father's illness was diagnosed as terminal and he was hospitalized, she had time to explain to her second-grade class before she flew home why she would be away for a while.

Her mother's death was sudden, and she did not get to talk with her class before leaving. But a friend, who substituted for her both times, explained the situation to the children.

On the teacher's first morning back, she was greeted by a little girl who hurried to her desk, put her arm around her teacher's shoulders, patted her gently, and said in a simple, childlike way, "That's the way the cookie crumbles."

Then without another word, the little girl went to her seat, took a book from her desk, and began to read.

Sometimes when we attempt to express comfort or sympathy for others in times of distress, sorrow, or bereavement, we try too hard. As Franz Schubert reminds us, "No one can really understand the grief or joy of another." We strive to express our innermost feelings, but words either refuse to come or sound stilted. We find ourselves stammering, faltering, and in the end, feeling frustrated because what we eventually say does not convey our true sentiments or sympathies.

"That's the way the cookie crumbles." The little girl's words, the way she spoke them in her sincere childish voice, her arm around her friend's shoulder, and her gentle pat all conveyed her understanding, her sympathy, her love, her concern, her desire to let her teacher know she cared. Then it became a closed matter; nothing more needed to be said.

C. H. Parkhurst expressed this thought beautifully by saying, "Sympathy is two hearts tugging at one load."

"The dew of compassion is a tear," the poet Byron tells us.

"Next to love," Edmund Burke said, "sympathy is the divinest passion of the human heart."

Now before the feast of the Passover, when Jesus knew that his hour was come that he should depart out of this world unto the Father, having loved his own which were in the world, he loved them unto the end.

"Let not your heart be troubled," Jesus told His disciples gathered about Him in the upper room. "Ye believe in God, believe also in me. In my Father's house are many mansions: if it were not so, I would have told you. I go to prepare a place for you. And if I go and prepare a place for you, I will come again, and receive you unto myself; that where I am, there ye may be also" (John 13:1; 14:1-3).

To pattern our lives after Jesus, we must conscientiously strive to cultivate compassion, tenderness, and sympathy for others, remembering how, through His life, Jesus showed compassion on crowds as well as individuals.

"There never was any heart truly great and generous, that was not also tender and compassionate," Robert South wrote in one of his sermons about 1650. Nearly a hundred years later, William Cowper gave us this thought: "Man may dismiss compassion from his heart, but God will never."

"Come unto me, all ye that labor and are heavy laden, and I will give you rest (Matthew 11:28). . . . Lo, I am with you alway, even unto the end of the world (Matthew 28:20). . . . Let not your heart be troubled (John 14:1). . . ." With such words of comfort and assurance, how can we fail to go out of our way to show love, tenderness, compassion, and sympathy for strangers as well as acquaintances and friends?

Closing Hymn: The Church's One Foundation

Closing Thought

"Real education should educate us out of self into something far finer—into a selflessness which links us with all humanity," wrote Lady Nancy Aster, the first woman to sit in the British House of Commons.

We might interpret her meaningful statement in the light of religious education and say, real religion should educate us out of self into something finer—into a selflessness which links us with all humanity.

Nothing Is Too Good for a Friend

Be thou an example of the believers, in word, in conversation, in charity, in spirit, in faith, in purity (1 Timothy 4:12).

∧∧∧∧∧∧∧∧∧∧∧∧∧∧∧∧∧∧∧∧∧∧∧∧∧∧∧∧∧∧∧∧∧∧∧∧∧∧

Opening Meditation

May constant desire for knowledge lead us to wisdom.
May increased wisdom lead us to sympathetic understanding.
May sympathetic understanding lead us to unexcelled tolerance.
And may tolerance, manifested toward all,
Exemplify our love for God.

Opening Hymn: Jesus Saves

Devotional

One day while in line at the post office to purchase stamps, Mrs. Vonk noticed a charming elderly lady in front of her. She held a handful of letters, addressed in a steady, clear, round script, indicating that each character had been formed with great care. While waiting, she shuffled through the envelopes as if double-checking each addresss. As she handled the envelopes, Mrs. Vonk detected a fragrant scent of lilacs.

Finally it was the lady's turn.

"What kind of stamps have you today?" she inquired of the postal clerk. "I don't want any of those faded, washed-out purple ones you sold me last week. Do you have something bright and pretty and lively?"

The postal clerk quickly recovered from his surprise and replied in much the same tone and manner a salesman in a department store would use to show a customer some expensive silver.

"Well, now, let's see what we have for you this morning. How about these?" And he showed her a sheet of stamps.

The little lady gave them a quick glance and with a wave of her hand said, "I don't like them. They're too cluttered."

"Well, what about these?" he asked as he showed her another sheet of stamps. "How do you like them?"

"Well—they're a little better, but they're not exactly what I had in mind. There's too much white in the background," she told him. "Is that all you have?"

"No, I have other stamps. How about these?" And he displayed still another sheet.

The lady's face lit up. "They're beautiful!" she exclaimed. "I'll take ten of them please."

With everyone watching, the lady placed a stamp on each envelope in a most painstaking manner. Then, after carefully checking each address once more, she deposited them, one by one, in the appropriate mailing slot. Only the best was good enough for her friends!

Friendships are, indeed, among our most valuable possessions. A life without friends is not only lonely and empty; it has been denied many treasured memories of happy moments spent in mutual understanding.

Friendships do not come to us automatically. They must be earned—deserved. Ralph Waldo Emerson said, "The only way to have a friend is to be one." (Read the parable of the sower, Luke 8:5-8.)

Throughout our lives we are sowing seeds. Seeds of love. Seeds of kindness. Seeds of understanding. Seeds of compassion. Seeds of encouragement. Seeds of friendship (speaking only of the positive seeds). But it's not enough merely to plant a seed. The seed must be nourished and tended in order for it to grow and in time yield a harvest.

No one has the monopoly on friendships. They must be two-way in nature. They must be giving as well as taking. They must be shared. They cannot be traded or imposed on others. True friendship cannot be bought. It must be deserved.

A class of first graders were asked what they would like to be when they grew up. One boy said, "First I'm going to be a golf pro like Arnie Palmer. Then I'm going to play baseball with one of the major leagues. Then I'm going to have a band of my own. Then I'm going into business with my father. And if I have any time left over, I'm going to college."

Another boy in the class said, "When I grow up, I'm going to be a friend."

"A friend to whom?" his teacher asked.

"Why, to everybody!" he exclaimed.

As these two illustrations show, even at first-grade level, children are beginning to develop a philosophy of life. A friend to everybody! What an exciting challenge for life!

Closing Hymn: O for a Closer Walk With God

Closing Thought

Make Me a Better Friend

Dear Lord, make me a better friend.
Not just today. Not just to those
I love and who love me. Not just
To those who might do me some good,
Or raise me to a higher state.
Help me be a better friend
To those with whom I live and work.
Help me to lend a ready hand
In times of sickness and distress.
Help me to be the first to share
In any trouble of a friend.
Help me to be that "friend in need"
Who proves himself "a friend in deed."
And when good fortune smiles upon
A friend, may I be first
To give my true congratulations
With honest heart, without the
Slightest trace of envy or jealousy.
Dear Lord, make me a better friend.
Through my loyalty to those
With whom I live on earth, may I
In some small way prove worthy here
Of Him whose everlasting loyalty
Makes Him the Friend of friends to all.

A Lesson in Patriotism

Blessed is the nation whose God is the Lord; and the people whom he hath chosen for his own inheritance (Psalm 33:12).

~~~~~~

Opening Meditation

Our Native Land
To every man the hills of home are best.
To each the mountains of his native land
Are loftier, the valleys far more fair;
The rivers wider, deeper, and every bank
An arboretum. The sun, the moon, the stars
Are never quite so radiant as when
They shine upon the land a man calls "home."
To every man his native land is best.

But those of us who have been privileged
To have been born Americans, or who
Have chosen these United States as an
Adopted native land, have every right
To look with swelling pride upon this as
The greatest country in the world today.
God has richly blessed our land,
But with such blessings come grave responsi-
    bilities—
To hold aloft the torch of freedom
As a symbol of our steadfast faith in God
And our unrestricted love for fellow men.

Opening Hymn: America the Beautiful

Devotional

Among the 1961-1962 refugees from Cuba were a newspaper editor and his wife, who had taught school in Havana.

Señora C, as the children called her, was a beautiful woman, always attractively clad. She was engaged as the Spanish teacher in a private school in Coral Gables, Florida, and came to the school daily to teach conversational Spanish to the children.

One day, Señora C was teaching the proper use of the Spanish

61

word for *pretty*. She had advanced the class far enough so that the children could speak simple sentences in Spanish. As she called their names, each child spoke an original sentence such as "My dress is pretty." "Her dress is pretty." "The book is pretty." Finally one boy pointed to the American flag displayed in front of the room and said, in Spanish, "The flag is pretty."

Instantly, Señora C sat erect, every nerve alive, her dark eyes flashing. She began breathing rapidly. The veins in her neck protruded, so violent were her heart palpitations.

"No, girls and boys," she practically shouted. "The American flag is *not* pretty!"

A death-like silence fell upon the classroom as the children looked at one another, and the teacher at the back of the room prayed for wisdom to cope with she knew not what.

"Boys and girls," Señora C continued with a decisiveness in her voice, "look at your flag!" All heads turned in that direction. "The American flag is *not pretty.*"

There was something almost reverent about her attitude as she continued.

"Girls and boys, the American flag is not *pretty!* The American flag is BEAUTIFUL. All of you stand up! Look at your flag! Say from the bottom of your heart, 'The American flag is BEAUTIFUL.' "

What a lesson in pride and respect!

What a lesson in patriotism!

"The name of *AMERICAN,* which belongs to you, in your national capacity, must always exalt the just pride of Patriotism," wrote George Washington at the founding of our great country. Decades later, Charles F. Browne wrote, "We can't all be Washingtons, but we can all be patriots and behave ourselves in a human and Christian manner."

Righteousness exalteth a nation: but sin is a reproach to any people.

We will rejoice in thy salvation, and in the name of our God we will set up our banners.

Some trust in chariots, and some in horses: but we will remember the name of the Lord our God.

Let the people praise thee, O God; let all the people praise thee.

O let the nations be glad and sing for joy: for thou shalt judge the people righteously, and govern the nations upon earth.

(Proverbs 14:34; Psalms 20:5, 7; 67:3, 4)

Closing Hymn: America

Closing Thought

Love for one's homeland is the axis around which revolves love for all peoples everywhere, regardless of which corners of the earth they proudly claim as their native lands. Three great women left us a legacy of challenging thoughts pertaining to patriotism.

Edith Louisa Cavell, an English nurse who died a martyr in World War I, wrote shortly before her death, "I realize that patriotism is not enough. I must have no hatred or bitterness toward anyone."

Jane Addams, an American social worker who founded the celebrated Hull House in the slums of Chicago, wrote, "Unless our conception of patriotism is progressive, it cannot hope to embody the real affection and the real interest of the nation."

Helen Adams Keller, the outstanding example of a person who conquered physical handicaps, wrote, "I look upon the whole world as my fatherland, and every war was to me a horror of a family feud. I look upon true patriotism as the brotherhood of man and the service of all to all."

Turning Disaster Into Opportunity

Wisdom is the principal thing; therefore get wisdom: and with all thy getting get understanding (Proverbs 4:7).

~~~~~~

Opening Meditation

Only Today Is Ours
Opportunities are like the hours of the day.
They appear but once within our span of life.
An hour spent can never be recalled;
The same holds true of opportunities.
Those opportunities that came with yesterday,
With yesterday passed out of our lives forever.
The precious hours of "now" are all we have.
So opportunities for service we ignore today are lost,
And shall remain forever lost to us.

Opening Hymn: Tell It Wherever You Go

Devotional

Every Friday after school, the first-grade teacher arranged a bulletin-board display of the pictures painted by the children in her class that week.

On Monday morning as the children entered the classroom, they hurried to the bulletin board and proudly identified their master-pieces. By Wednesday, they looked at the bulletin board from their seats (if they looked at it at all), as the display had by that time become a part of the classroom decor. By Friday they were ready for the new bulletin board that would be awaiting them the next Monday morning.

But one particular week, Janie hurried to the bulletin board every morning when she arrived and stood for a few seconds admiring her picture (so the teacher thought) before taking her seat. Now, Janie was not one of the class artists. Although she thoroughly enjoyed working with all art media, her results were always cluttered and messy. So, as the teacher noticed Janie's continued interest in the bulletin board, naturally, she was pleased.

Then on Friday morning, after Janie had made her trip to the bulletin board upon her arrival, she marched up to the teacher and said reproachfully, "Mrs. Vonk, my picture has been hanging upside down all week, and you didn't even notice it!"

It was not until then that Mrs. Vonk recalled puzzling over the picture before hanging it, holding it one way and then another, trying to decide which was up and which was down. Only Janie could tell the difference.

Here was a child who had nursed a secret disappointment all week—and a week is a long time in the life of a child. She had done her work as usual and had shown no signs of resentment—yet all the while she was sensing a deep hurt inside. As Mrs. Vonk looked at the child in distress, she had a brilliant idea.

"Janie," she said, "your picture is a very interesting one. A very special one. Before I hung it on the bulletin board, I noticed that it was just as pretty hanging upside down as it was right side up. Now, if you will look at all the other pictures, you'll see that they all can be hung only one way—right side up. But your picture, Janie, can be hung right side up or upside down, and it's pretty either way."

Janie blossomed at these words of praise, and the wise teacher seized the opportunity to spotlight Janie's art and at the same time to teach another lesson.

That afternoon, using Janie's picture as an example, the children created design pictures that could be hung both ways—right side up and upside down. The project proved an interesting, creative one for all.

In the words of William Penn, "Opportunities should never be lost, because they can hardly be regained." O. L. Grothingham advised, "Let not the opportunity that is so fleeting, yet so full, pass neglected away."

"Some of us miss opportunity because we are too dull to try. Others let opportunity go by, too much startled when they see it to take hold of it," Arthur Brisbane, an American journalist, observed.

According to W. E. Dunning, "Great opportunities come to all, but many do not know they have met them."

Recognizing an opportunity when it confronts us requires wisdom, and wisdom requires understanding. Perhaps there is no better single collection of pithy maxims concerning the value of obtaining wisdom and understanding than we find in the book of Proverbs.

The Lord giveth wisdom: out of his mouth cometh knowledge and understanding (Proverbs 2:6).

Trust in the Lord with all thine heart; and lean not unto thine own understanding (Proverbs 3:5).

Happy is the man that findeth wisdom, and the man that getteth understanding *(Proverbs 3:13)*.

Get wisdom, get understanding: forget it not *(Proverbs 4:5)*.

The fear of the Lord is the beginning of wisdom: and the knowledge of the Holy is understanding *(Proverbs 9:10)*.

He that is void of wisdom despiseth his neighbour: but a man of understanding holdeth his peace *(Proverbs 11:12)*.

Closing Hymn: Open My Eyes That I May See

Closing Thought

Get Oil for Your Lamp

Come and get oil for your lamp
Through diligently seeking more wisdom
And more understanding.
More oil in your lamp means brighter light.
Brighter light means more light shed upon the way.
More light shed upon the way not only means more
    pleasant traveling for yourself,
      but for all those who walk beside you
      and all those who will follow close behind.
"Get wisdom, get understanding: forget it not."

Consistency

Jesus Christ the same yesterday, and today, and for ever (Hebrews 13:8).

~~~~~~

Opening Meditation

Let the Beauty of Christ Be Upon Us
Let the beauty of Christ be upon us.
Let the beauty of Christ enter in us.
Let the beauty of Christ radiate from within us:
So our deeds may illumine the pathways of others,
So our words may give light unto all who are lost,
So our prayers may evolve from our reverence and love,
So that others may see our steadfastness as we
    follow Him,
And through us may be led to the beauty of Christ.

Opening Hymn: Since Jesus Came Into My Heart

Devotional

During recess one afternoon the week before Easter, the teacher noticed her second graders in a cluster near the deserted swings, apparently engrossed in serious discussion. So she was not surprised when, as soon as they had had their drinks and were back in the classroom, she was asked, "Mrs. Vonk, is there an Easter bunny?"

Mrs. Vonk thought a minute, then asked, "How many of you believe there's an Easter bunny?"

One boy promptly raised his hand while the rest of the children shouted, "Dale!" and pointed in his direction.

Dale was an interesting child. A good student. The eldest of two boys of a fairly young couple. His teeth were so soft and so vulnerable to decay that all forms of sugar had to be eliminated from his diet. He could not eat cookies, cake, frosting, candy, or any of the other sweets most children enjoy. His dentist had sent a note to the school dietitian and one to the teacher requesting that they observe such restrictions. Dale had been well informed and accepted such restrictions without complaint.

Looking at him, the teacher asked, "Dale, do you believe there's an Easter bunny?"

"I *know* there's an Easter bunny," he said emphatically.

"Have you ever seen the Easter bunny?" she asked.

"No," he replied, "but I *know* there's an Easter bunny."

"How do you know there's an Easter bunny?" Mrs. Vonk pursued.

"Well," he explained, "Mrs. Vonk, *you* know about my teeth. *You* know I can't have any candy. My *mother* knows about my teeth. My *father* knows about my teeth. My *grandmother* knows about my teeth. But every Easter morning I find a basket of chocolate eggs under my bed. Now my mother wouldn't give me candy. My father wouldn't give me candy. My grandmother wouldn't give me candy. But there's that basket of chocolate eggs under my bed. So there *has* to be an Easter bunny that brings me candy because he doesn't know about my teeth."

Apparently Dale's parents felt receiving an Easter basket of chocolate eggs such an important part of childhood that once a year they were willing to violate the restrictions made for his own good and to which they adhered faithfully except at Easter. Obviously they were so consistent in every other respect that it was easier for Dale to believe in the existence of an Easter bunny than in such inconsistency on the part of his parents or grandmother.

One of the cardinal rules when dealing successfully with children or teens (or even with adults) is to exercise consistency in all matters at all times. Inconsistency—like forbidding a certain activity one day and permitting it the next—confuses teens as well as children. So does prohibiting participation in some event one day and granting permission the next. Or saying no to a request today and yes to the same request tomorrow. Or punishing one day and ignoring the same act the next day. Such inconsistencies confuse the growing child and the searching youth.

But more than that, inconsistencies manifest an adult who is not fully mature, does not know her own mind, has not formulated opinions and convictions concerning important matters, and lacks strength of character to stand firmly for what she believes is right.

Inconsistencies in the home, at school, and in society at large are responsible for much of the unnecessary bewilderment and confusion experienced by many children and young people—and all too frequently, by adults, too. Inconsistency destroys confidence, for, as Franklin Roosevelt so aptly said, "Confidence strives on honesty, on honor, on the sacredness of obligation, on faithful protection, and on unselfish performance. Without them it cannot live."

The writer of the letter to the Hebrews assured them of the consistency of Jesus. "Jesus Christ," he wrote, "the same yesterday, and today, and for ever" *(Hebrews 13:8).*

The consistency of Jesus is our rainbow, our North Star, our alpha and omega. We are promised that to the end of time, Jesus will be the way, the truth, and the life for all who believe. Throughout eternity, we have His assurance that none will come to the Father except through Him. What greater assurance can we desire than the steadfastness, the consistency, and the never-changing Word of God?

Closing Hymn: Faith of Our Fathers

Closing Meditation

Lord Keep Us Faithful

In the radiant hours of early dawn when the whole world
Is freshly bathed with glistening dew,
And life seems beautiful, and friends steadfast and true,
It is not hard to prove our faithfulness;
Nor when the answers to our prayers are realized
Almost before the prayer leaves our lips;
Nor when prosperity appoints us favorite child,
Directing streams of blessings to our door;
Nor when the crowd applauds us hero of the hour.

But on the mornings when the sun withdraws its warmth
And cold, gray shadows turn the day to night;
When trouble beats his ruthless fists upon our door,
And others seem far greater blessed than we;
When disappointments, actual want, or faithless friends
Descend upon us like torrential rain;
Or when our prayers appear rejected or unheard;
O Lord, may each of us prove faithful even then!
Pray, give us the courage, Lord, which comes
From being faithful to Thee to the end.

The Art of Conversation

I say unto you, That every idle word that men shall speak, they shall give account thereof in the day of judgment. For by thy words thou shalt be justified, and by thy words thou shalt be condemned (Matthew 12:36, 37).

Opening Meditation

The True Worshiper
It is so easy to get lost in this world—
To become absorbed by the crowd—
To drift along with the current of time—
Forgetting all else but material gains—
Laboring only for temporal things.
The true worshiper is she who holds
The love of God within her heart,
And daily comes before her Lord
With deep-found reverence and love.

Opening Hymn: Tell Me the Story of Jesus

Devotional

It is always desirable for a hostess to know the plans of a house guest in order to be able to arrange meals, trips, and whatever else might be involved in making the visit as pleasant as possible for all concerned. One way to find out how long your guests plan to stay is to ask, "When are you leaving?" Another way is to ask, "How long can you be with us?" There's a world of difference between those two seemingly casual questions. The difference lies in the choice of words.

"When are you leaving?" lacks warmth and congeniality. The words convey a hint that hopefully the visit will be a short one. "How long can you be with us?" radiates cordial hospitality. The words suggest the hope of a reasonably long, pleasant stay.

The ability to be articulate and to carry on a conversation with ease seems to come naturally for some individuals. For others, conversation is a painful experience. Many children develop the art of conversation by the time they enter school. Mike, a first grader who took a trip around the world with his parents, is an example.

Mike had developed an uncanny memory and an exceptionally keen power of observation for a five-year-old. He was able to recall in detail many exciting experiences afforded by the tour. Hardly a day passed without something being said in the afternoon discussion period that caused his thoughts to leap suddenly across the globe. When he began, "That reminds me of the time—" everybody listened intently; for Mike, using only words, painted vivid, colorful pictures of skiing in the Alps, gliding down the canals of Venice in a gondola, visiting flower markets in the Netherlands, riding on a camel over the African sand.

One of the keys to developing into an interesting conversationalist is to strengthen our powers of observation, to open our eyes and ears to what is going on about us. We must reinforce the memory so that we can store for future recall the beautiful sights we see, and the wonderful sounds we hear.

But conversation has its danger zones. Words are indispensable tools for conveying our thoughts. Words are also sharp instruments that can cut deeply. What we say and how we say it can have a lasting good or damaging effect on the person or persons to whom our words are spoken. As a warning in this direction, Edward Everett wrote, "Words once spoken can never die; they will turn up on the day of judgment, like things in life, and will either acquit or condemn." An ancient philosopher reminds us that once words are spoken, they can never be recalled.

The Bible presents a fascinating study of the power and use of words by describing many types. Would that time and space permitted us to delve more deeply, but suffice it to consider a few examples found in the New Testament.

Simple Words

So likewise ye, except ye utter by the tongue words easy to be understood, how shall it be known what is spoken? for ye shall speak into the air (1 Corinthians 14:9).

Words of Deception

Let no man deceive you with vain words: for because of these things cometh the wrath of God upon the children of disobedience (Ephesians 5:6).

Words of Enticement

And this I say, lest any man should beguile you with enticing words (Colossians 2:4).

Words of Flattery

For neither at any time used we flattering words, as ye know, nor

a cloke of covetousness: God is witness *(1 Thessalonians 2:5)*.
Words of Comfort
Wherefore comfort one another with these words *(1 Thessalonians 4:18)*.
Words of Faith and Good Doctrine
If thou put the brethren in remembrance of these things, thou shalt be a good minister of Jesus Christ, nourished up in the words of faith and of good doctrine, whereunto thou hast attained *(1 Timothy 4:6)*.
Wholesome Words
If any man teach otherwise, and consent not to wholesome words, even the words of our Lord Jesus Christ, and to the doctrine which is according to godliness; he is proud, knowing nothing, but doting about questions and strifes of words, whereof cometh envy, strife, railings, evil surmisings *(1 Timothy 6:3, 4)*.
Sound Words
Hold fast the form of sound words, which thou hast heard of me, in faith and love which is in Christ Jesus *(2 Timothy 1:13)*.
Feigned Words
And through covetousness shall they with feigned words make merchandise of you *(2 Peter 2:3, 4)*.
Words of Vanity
For when they speak great swelling words of vanity, they allure through the lusts of the flesh, through much wantonness, those that were clean escaped from them who live in error *(2 Peter 2:18)*.
Faithful and True Words
And he that sat upon the throne said, Behold, I make all things new. And he said unto me, Write: for these words are true and faithful *(Revelation 21:5)*.

Closing Hymn: Wonderful Words of Life

Closing Thought

God is love.
So he who keeps love in his heart
Keeps God there, too.

The Signs of Well-Adjustment

Well done, thou good and faithful servant: thou hast been faithful over a few things, I will make thee ruler over many things (Matthew 25:21).

‹‹

Opening Meditation

God has been very good to each of us.
He has given us physical blessings too numerous to count.
Our eyes, our ears, our hands, our feet—
The power to think, to speak, to feel, to love.
God has given each of us specific talents to use or
waste, according to our will.
How bountifully the Lord has blessed each one of us.
May our lives reflect the depths of our gratitude to Him.

Opening Hymn: Willing Am I

Devotional

Philip was seven years old and in the second grade. His father had entered Harvard at the age of fifteen, graduated with honors, and was a prominent attorney. Phillip's mother had a masters degree in American Literature and had devoted many hours introducing Philip to the wonderful world of books. It was little wonder that he was a very precocious child. (The word *precocious* comes from the Latin *praecox* meaning "ripening before its time.")

Philip was exceptionally tall for a second grader and would have fitted perfectly in any accelerated third-grade class. He was too advanced for second grade as the work on the level offered him no challenge. The school, however, did not approve of a child's "skipping a grade," so Philip was obliged to remain in the second grade until that policy was altered in his favor, and he was promoted to the third grade in the middle of the first semester.

On the first day of school his teacher realized that it would be imperative to plan something each day that would challenge Philip, keep him interested in school, and excited about learning.

On the third day, Philip himself gave her the answer. He entered the classroom, early as usual, exuberating the joy of learning. He went straight to Mrs. Vonk's desk and asked, in his bubbling way,

"Mrs. Vonk, what are we going to teach the children today?"

And that is exactly what they did during the next three weeks until Philip was promoted to the third grade. They taught the children together—Philip and the teacher. It was a wonderful experience for all of them—for Philip, for the other children, and for the teacher.

Well-adjustment doesn't just happen. It cannot be bought, nor can it be borrowed or loaned. It must be developed by degrees. Individuals, regardless of age, who know that they have been endowed with a superior mind or with special talents have a responsibility to use such gifts in ways that will benefit society and glorify God.

In the words of Jesus, "For unto whomsoever much is given, of him shall be much required; and to whom men have committed much, of him they will ask the more" (Luke 12:48).

Scott Nearing said, "Maladjustment is darkness. Adjustment is light." Yet in our present-day society, we hear more about the maladjusted than we hear about the well-adjusted, even though the great majority of individuals are well-adjusted. Individuals who can honestly evaluate their own strengths and their own weaknesses, not only in a physical sense but in all areas of life, including abilities, talents, potentials, and limitations, remain well-adjusted. Those who cannot are apt to become maladjusted because they do not understand their capabilities, and either expect too little or too much of themselves.

But willingness to assume responsibility according to our potential must be related to God. "The most important thought I ever had was that of my individual responsibility to God," Daniel Webster wrote. When we sense our individual responsibility to God, we will also sense our individual responsibility to our fellowmen.

J. G. Holland has given us this challenging thought: "Responsibility walks hand in hand with capacity and power."

Gail Hamilton, an American writer, expressed these thoughts by saying, "Every person is responsible for all the good within the scope of his abilities, and for no more, and none can tell whose sphere is the largest."

(Read Matthew 25:14-30.)

This parable of the talents contains four parts:

1. The great kindness of the master who, according to his own will, distributed the talents among his servants.

2. The servants who showed trustworthiness and appreciation to their master by improving their gifts.

3. The servant who made no use of his talent, but buried it.

4. The punishment of the unworthy servant.

Speaking of the good seed in the parable of the sower, Jesus said, "But other (seeds) fell into good ground, and brought forth fruit, some a hundredfold, some sixtyfold, some thirtyfold" *(Matthew 13:8).*

May we ever strive to be a good seed, a workman that needeth not to be ashamed.

Closing Hymn: Work for the Night Is Coming

Closing Thought

Are You Using All Your Talents?
God has given each of us abilities and talents,
Some of which lie deeply buried in our lives;
So deeply buried that we are completely
Unaware that they exist.
When least expected, they appear and
Lift our work from ordinary spheres
To some distinguished height.
We would never know such talents
If we had not been willing to exert our best efforts
And give the best of self to the task at hand.
So often talents lie unused and, therefore, wasted,
Just because the one to whom they have been given
Fails to do her best.

It Takes Time to Mature

Be ye steadfast (1 Corinthians 15:58).

〰〰〰〰〰〰〰〰〰〰〰〰〰〰〰〰〰〰〰〰〰〰〰〰〰〰

Opening Meditation

Trust in the Lord,
Have faith in His Word;
For the Lord is your strength in times of weakness.
He is your hope in times of doubt.
He is your light in times of bewilderment.
He is your refuge in times of discouragement.
He is your teacher.
Your light,
Your friend.
Trust in the Lord,
Have faith in His Word.

Opening Hymn: Beneath the Cross of Jesus

Devotional

Denny was a slow reader. Because he was six years old, he was placed in the first grade even though he was very immature for his age. Denny was anxious to learn to read, but he simply could not remember the difference between the shapes of letters, the sounds of letters, or even simple words like *see* and *go*.

Then one day after months of working with seeming little progress, Denny opened a preprimer at random. His eyes lit upon the word *us*. His face beamed. He pointed his finger at the word and proudly exclaimed, "I saw that word on TV last night! Only it had an *A* behind it!"

At last he saw and recognized and remembered some letters! It would have been difficult to say whose excitement was the greater over his wonderful discovery—Denny's or his teacher's. He was like a child living in a dark room, groping for something to shed light, then suddenly touching the light switch and being showered by a bright, comforting glow.

How often we are Dennys, trying to accomplish tasks for which we are not ready. Asking for blessings involving situations only to find ourselves too immature or too inexperienced to handle the blessings when we receive them. Groping for the switch that will give us the light of understanding, the gleam of knowledge, the patience to wait upon the Lord.

We forget that Rome wasn't built in a day. Maturity is not realized overnight. Just as there are many stages from the blossom to the ripened fruit, so there are many stages in our personal growth and development. It is better to be patient, and attempt challenging tasks by degrees, than to plunge into the middle of a situation only to find we were not ready for the accompanying responsibilities or the pressures involved.

A first grader, referring to the ability to jump rope, informed her teacher on the playground one recess, "Long ago when I was young, I couldn't do that. But now I can."

In His infinite wisdom, God surrounded us with opportunities for personal growth and development. Opportunities to mature physically, intellectually, and spiritually. But as Calvin Coolidge so aptly said, "All growth depends upon activity. There is no development physically or intellectually without effort, and effort means work."

This is certainly true of our spiritual growth as well. We must work as diligently, as conscientiously, and as faithfully, striving to understand the Word of God, as little Denny worked to understand the letters of the alphabet.

We are told to seek knowledge, seek understanding. We are not told to hold out our hands, and they will be given to us. The harder we seek—the more diligently we study the Scriptures—the more light will be shed upon our efforts, and the greater spiritual growth we will enjoy.

The story is told of two traveling men who were forced to share a motel room as the result of an unexpected snowstorm. Before the one retired, he took from his briefcase his Bible and Bible commentary. He read first from the Bible and then from the commentary, studying each verse in turn. After a half hour of serious study, he closed both books, closed his eyes, and felt the blessings of close communion with God through silent prayer.

The other man knelt beside his bed, closed his eyes, folded his hands, and said aloud, "Now I lay me down to sleep. I pray Thee, Lord, my soul to keep. If I should die before I wake, I pray Thee, Lord, my soul to take."

What a difference in the spiritual growth of these two men! The one had not grown since early childhood. The other was enjoying the great blessing of close communion with God.

Closing Hymn: Let Jesus Come Into Your Heart

Closing Thought

As Jesus sought quiet moments with His Father,
  so must we,
As Jesus took time to pray to His Father,
  so must we,
As Jesus lived by the Scriptures,
  so must we,
If we would enjoy the great blessing
  of close communion with God.

Meeting the Needs of Others

Let every man prove his own work, and then shall he have rejoicing in himself alone, and not in another (Galatians 6:4).

∿∿∿

Opening Meditation

Walking With God

Blessed are those who walk with God;
Who feel God's presence on the earth;
Who see God's glory in the skies;
Who pause each day to quietly commune with God
And thank Him for His wondrous love
   from which all blessings flow.
Blessed are those who walk with God,
For in such hearts abide both peace and love
So great and endless they overflow
Into the lives of others,
Bringing joy and comfort,
Cheer and happiness
   all along life's way.

Opening Hymn: Holy, Holy, Holy

Devotional

Jimmy was a sixth grader, reading on low second-grade level. He hated books, and he hated everybody who had anything to do with books. No matter how his reading teacher tried, he would not respond to anything she said.

One Friday morning as Jimmy came into the room, his teacher tried again.

"Good morning, Jimmy," she said cheerfully. "Today's Friday! That means there's another wonderful weekend before us!"

"I hate weekends," he replied.

"Jimmy, you're the only boy I've ever met who hates weekends," the teacher said, hoping to prolong the conversation.

"Well, not the whole weekend. Just Sundays," he said.

"Why do you hate Sundays?" the teacher asked.

"Well, it's really not Sundays. I hate church."

"Why do you hate church?"

"Well, it's really not church. It's Bible school. I hate Bible school."

Then, little by little, he revealed the cause of his negative feelings. His was a Christian family; every member attended Bible school and church every Sunday. Jimmy's Bible-school teacher, a dedicated, sincere individual, wanted each child to participate during the lesson period in order to feel an important part of the group; so she had each read in turn a verse of Scripture from the King James Version.

Jimmy was not ready to handle the King James Version, as beautiful as it is. In fact, at that time, Jimmy was not ready to handle any version of the Bible, even one written in the simplest form for children. Every Sunday morning he agonized during the lesson period, for the other children had to feed him every word when it was his turn to read. His frustration was so great he couldn't even read the few small words he knew. This made him appear stupid in the eyes of his peers—and children are quick to notice and long to remember such incompetencies. Poor Jimmy. He must have died a hundred deaths each Sunday morning.

Perhaps we ought to give some thought to whether at times we try too hard to make everyone a part of the group. Try too hard to make everyone feel at ease. Try too hard to cheer a friend who has suffered a loss. Forgetting that we are each different from all others. Some like to listen. Some like to talk. Some like to participate. Some like to observe. Do we sometimes try so hard to fill the needs of others that we become blinded to their greatest need? If such is true of a teacher, can it not also be true of a parent? Of a friend?

> Bless, O Lord, this food to our use,
> And us to Thy service.
> Make us ever mindful
> Of the needs of others.

This simple mealtime prayer keeps us aware that each of us has individual needs. We need but recall a few of the miracles to appreciate how Christ met the many and varied needs of those who were among the crowds listening to His teaching, and those He met along the roads while traveling from one place to another.

In Matthew 9:27-30, we read how Christ recognized the individual needs of the two blind men and restored their sight. In Matthew 9:32, 33, is recorded the healing of the dumb demoniac. Christ ministered to individual needs by raising the widow's son from the dead *(Luke 7:11-15);* healing the woman's deformed body *(Luke 13:11-13);* healing the man with dropsy *(Luke 14:1-5);* healing the ten lepers *(Luke 17:11-19),* to cite but a few.

All of Christ's teachings and all of His ministry were on an individual basis to take care of individual needs.

Dear Father, make us ever mindful
Of the needs of others.

Closing Hymn: Living for Jesus

Closing Thought

Be faithful and dedicated,
And God shall reward you
With a song in your heart,
A smile on your face,
Serenity of mind,
And peace of soul,
So that you may have the wisdom
To sense the needs of others,
And the compassion to do your part
In fulfilling such needs.

Too Much of a Good Thing

And every man that striveth for the mastery is temperate in all things (1 Corinthians 9:25).

~~~~~~

Opening Meditation

Be Silent Now and Wait
God speaks to each of us.
Quiet your troubled soul,
Silence your doubting fears,
And still your restless mind
So you can listen for
His gentle, loving voice,
And hear Him speak your name.
Be silent now and wait
Upon the Lord,
For He is here and
Waiting just for you.

Opening Hymn: Be Still My Soul

Devotional

It was St. Patrick's Day, and the school dietitian had been generous with the green food coloring. There were fried chicken legs, hot rolls, kelly green mashed potatoes, yellow green butter patties, and cupcakes with light green frosting.

Any teacher could have predicted what was about to happen. The children ate the fried chicken legs, they ate the hot rolls, they ate the green peas and the green frosted cupcakes. But they left the green mashed potatoes and the greenish butter on their trays.

The same bottle of tasteless, green vegetable coloring had been used to color the mashed potatoes, the butter, and the frosting, but green mashed potatoes and greenish butter created a negative psychological effect on the children. They made faces and shook their heads as their teachers tried to convince them that mashed potatoes taste the same white or green.

On the other hand, the green frosting on the cupcakes created a positive psychological attitude; the children were accustomed to seeing and eating cake and cookies decorated with various colored frosting. They expected the frosting to taste good and, of course, it did.

The more immature we are, the more difficult it is for us to accept any deviation from the usual. We often hear adults use expressions such as, "I know there's no difference, *but—*" and then make a choice which is not always the wisest simply because they are afraid to try something new or different.

Robert L. Ripley observed that "people believe only in the commonplace, that which they are accustomed to see."

As we mature, we should be able to see beyond the surface, to recognize objects or situations for what they are, not for their outward appearances alone. In short, maturity should enable us to govern our psychological attitudes rather than permit our psychological attitudes to govern us.

The apostle Paul in his letter to the Philippians left us a beautiful piece of advice that is as timely today as it was when he wrote these words at the beginning of the Christian era:

Rejoice in the Lord always: and again I say, Rejoice.

Let your moderation be known unto all men. The Lord is at hand.

Be careful for nothing; but in every thing by prayer and supplication with thanksgiving let your requests be known unto God.

And the peace of God, which passeth all understanding, shall keep your hearts and minds through Christ Jesus (4:4-7).

After Jenny Lind, known internationally as the Swedish Nightingale, had been called so many times before the curtain after her brilliant performance in *Norma* that she was completely exhausted, she commented, "Everything should be done in moderation: otherwise it is not pleasing."

Charles Kingsley, noted author of Victorian England, left us a summary of excellent advice: "Thank God every morning when you get up that you have something to do which must be done, whether you like it or not. Being forced to work, and forced to do your best, will breed in you moderation, self-control, diligence, strength of will, content, and a hundred other virtues which the idle never know."

Closing Hymn: I Love Thy Kingdom, Lord

Closing Thought

> Whatsoever things are true,
> Whatsoever things are honest,
> Whatsoever things are just,
> Whatsoever things are pure,

Whatsoever things are lovely,
Whatsoever things are of good report;
If there be any virtue,
And if there be any praise,
Think on these things
(Philippians 4:8).

Performance Speaks for Itself

There is one body, and one Spirit, even as ye are called in one hope of your calling;
one Lord, one faith, one baptism, one God and Father of all, who is above all, and through all, and in you all.
But unto every one of us is given grace according to the measure of the gift of Christ (Ephesians 4:4-7).

∧∧

Opening Meditation

"If any man will come after me, let him deny himself, and take up his cross, and follow me.

For whosoever will save his life shall lose it: and whosoever will lose his life for my sake shall find it."

So spoke our Lord and Master, Jesus, to His disciples many centuries ago.

And so speaks our Lord and Master, Jesus, to His disciples even today.

Blessed are they who heed His Holy Word and follow His blessed example.

Opening Hymn: Just When I Need Him Most

Devotional

Two women were engaged in an animated discussion concerning the accomplishments of their respective daughters. Everything the first woman bragged her daughter could do, the second woman boasted her daughter could do better. Each woman seemed determined to convince the other that her daughter was the most talented, the most accomplished, and had the most promising future.

Finally, the first woman exclaimed, "My daughter can tap dance! In fact, she's a very good tap dancer!"

Not to be outdone, the second woman tossed back her head and said, "Why, I've paid out good money for tap-dancing lessons for my daughter for the last five years!"

Whereupon, the first woman took a step closer and glared at her, "Yes! But can she do it? Can she do it?" It was not enough to "pay out good money for tap-dancing lessons for the last five years." The question was had the girl achieved?

Being provided opportunities for growth in any area is not enough. We must make the most of every opportunity given us for self-development if we expect to attain a high degree of accomplishment.

We are each endowed with certain abilities. Many of these abilities will remain dormant until we are willing to give the time and discipline necessary to develop them.

Theodore Roosevelt left us this challenge: "We have got but one life here. . . . It pays, no matter what comes after it, to try and do things, to accomplish things in this life, and not merely to have a soft and pleasant time."

Two generations later, Franklin Delano Roosevelt wrote, "Happiness . . . lies in the joy of achievement, in the thrill of creative effort." When speaking of achievement, we might say, "The proof of the pudding is in the doing."

It is not enough to read our Bibles. We must make use of its teachings in our daily lives. It is not enough to go to church service on Sunday. We must worship and serve Christ throughout the week. It is not enough to support programs that bring Christ to our communities. We must support missionary efforts that help bring the story of Christ and His redeeming love to all people everywhere.

Wendel D. Craker, a contemporary minister, said, "There is something new in Heaven because Christ lived. The something new is redeemed humanity."

If our Christian performance is to speak favorably for us, we must be part of the effort to let those at home and in foreign lands who know not Christ understand that they, too, are a part of the redeemed humanity.

Paul's letters to the newly organized congregations are rich in words of enlightenment and encouragement. To the Christians at Rome, he wrote these words:

Having then gifts differing according to the grace that is given to us, whether prophecy, let us prophesy according to the proportion of faith;

Or ministry, let us wait on our ministering: or he that teacheth, on teaching;

Or he that exhorteth, on exhortation: he that giveth, let him do it with simplicity; he that ruleth, with diligence; he that showeth mercy, with cheerfulness (Romans 12:6-8).

Self-dedication is contagious. Many great Christian movements for humanity's good have developed out of the efforts of one dedicated person.

86

Closing Hymn: In the Garden

Closing Thought

Self-Dedication

No one can say to another,
"Go your own way and fear not.
For I love you.
And I will serve for you.
And in the end, I shall answer for you."
For to each of us has been given the power and the privilege to
   serve.
No one can serve for another even as
No one can eat for another.
God, in His all-wise and all-knowing way,
Created us as unlike as the blades of grass which carpet a hillside.
Then, in His infinite wisdom,
He created for us interminable ways of service.
Therefore, anyone who would serve may do so, regardless of
   person, or ability, or means, or talents.
But first we must seek the paths of service
Through self-accomplishment, striving ever to improve our per-
   formance,
And through self-dedication, striving ever to give our best.

Learning to Relax

Godliness with contentment is great gain (1 Timothy 6:6).

‸‸

Opening Meditation

Contentment

The secret of contentment lies in learning
To appreciate all gifts received.
Contentment, then, is born of gratitude.
Contentment frees the soul of envy, jealousy, and hatred.
Those who find only discontentment in the things they have
Will never be contented with those things they want
And which they feel are needed to assure their happiness.
For happiness consists, not in possessing worldly goods,
But in being contented with the things we possess.
Those who find naught but discontentment in this life
Are never rich, regardless of their material gains.
For happiness is contentment,
And contentment is born of gratitude.

Opening Hymn: Now Thank We All Our God

Devotional

The candy counter of a department store was a busy place. One couple had waited in line for several minutes. When it was finally their turn, the man pointed to some dark chocolates, but before he could give his order another man rushed up to the counter, pointed to some creams and snapped, "Quick! A pound of these! I want to catch the next elevator!"

The clerk eyed him for a moment in silence. Then in a very relaxed deliberate manner she leaned against her side of the counter, still gazing steadily at him. In a quiet but firm tone and with appropriate hand gestures, she said, "Mister, that elevator goes up and down, up and down all day long."

Then turning to the first man, she repeated, "May I help you?"

We sometimes become so obsessed with rushing through life that we don't take time to live. Many things—particularly the insignificant common, everyday courtesies—are pushed aside. Ignored. And in time, completely forgotten. We plow through life like the proverbial bull in the china shop, insensitive to the feelings, the conveniences, and frequently, even the rights of others. We all need a quiet but firm voice to remind us that the elevator goes up and down, up and down all day long.

Discontentment is one of the greatest barriers to being able to relax and enjoy our blessings. "A contented mind is the greatest blessing a man can enjoy in this world; and if, in the present life, his happiness arises from the subduing of his desires, it will arise in the next from the gratification of them," wrote Joseph Addison, the English poet.

Shakespeare has given us the immortal lines concerning contentment:

My crown is in my heart, not on my head;
Not deck'd with diamonds, and Indian stones,
Nor to be seen; my crown is called Content;
A crown it is that seldom kings enjoy.

Benjamin Franklin suggested two ways to find contentment: "We may either diminish our wants or augment our means—either will do—the result is the same; and it is for each man to decide for himself, and do that which happens to be the easiest."

Robert Louis Stevenson also outlined the attributes of a contented person: "To be honest, to be kind, to earn a little, and to spend a little less, to make upon the whole a family happier for his presence, to renounce when that shall be necessary and not to be embittered, to keep a few friends, but these without capitulation; above all, on the same condition, to keep friends with himself; here . . . is the contented man."

Luke's account of Christ's unexpected visit in the home of Mary and Martha depicts the ability of one to relax and the inability of the other. Complete contentment on the part of one and agitation stemming from discontentment on the part of the other. Martha, the woman who could not relax because there was work to do. Mary, the woman who was able to put first things first and enjoy the blessing of relaxation during Christ's brief visit.

When Martha, who was cumbered about much serving, came to Jesus, complaining that Mary had deserted her and that she was left to prepare the meal alone, Jesus must have looked at Martha with eyes filled with understanding and compassion. Perhaps He took her hand and patted it gently while He said, "Martha, Martha, thou art careful and troubled about many things: but one thing is needful; and Mary hath chosen that good part, which shall not be taken away from her" *(Luke 10:38-42)*.

There are times in our lives when we must be Marthas. Household demands must be met if our family life is to move along smoothly to the benefit of all concerned. But when we become solely Marthas, we are in danger of becoming like the man who was too rushed to wait for an elevator. When we take time to relax, realizing that the elevator goes up and down, up and down all day long, we not only find greater enjoyment in life; we become a blessing to all who know us.

Closing Hymn: More Love to Thee

Closing Thought

How blessed are the ones who love the Lord!
For He has given them the makings
Of a paradise right here on earth!
How can we be so foolish as to reject
A gift so rare, a blessing far too great
For the feeble power of man to understand?

So let us thank the Lord for His eternal gift
And as we bow in supplication and in prayer,
May we unite our hearts in proclamation of
    God's great glory,
And may our hearts respond to His wondrous love.

Mountains out of Molehills?

Follow peace with all men, and holiness, without which no man shall see the Lord (Hebrews 12:14).

^^

Opening Meditation

Prejudices

It is a grave mistake to set up standards of our own
Concerning what we think is wrong and what is right.
For who are we to set ourselves apart and be the judge?
And who are we to demand that others follow us
And like the things we like, and do the things we do?
And who are we to think ourselves the privileged ones
Superior to all the other people of the world?

Each prejudice invites intolerance.
Intolerance breeds hate, contempt, rejection, malice, and distrust.
It is for God, not mortals, to make the laws regarding
What is wrong and what is right. These laws concern
The whole of mankind, everywhere, without regard to creed.
When prejudices fill our lives, they make us blind
To the good that lies in fellow beings despite all differences.

Opening Hymn: Make Me a Blessing

Devotional

University professors have the privilege of teaching many exceptionally fine students. In most colleges, there is also a sprinkling of students who might be described as unusual—extremists—way-outs. They are so labeled because of their mannerisms, opinions, and/or attire. In Maxine's case, it was her hairstyling, or lack of it.

Maxine was a fairly good student, cooperative, intelligent, capable of attaining a high level of achievement when she applied herself and made the best use of her time and talents. But her hair always suggested an unsightly tangled mop.

On one day, however, Maxine looked different. On the day it was her turn to present a teaching unit she had prepared, she arrived early in order to arrange her materials. Mrs. Vonk also arrived early. That day Maxine looked perfectly stunning. Her hair was beautifully brushed in a most becoming style.

The contrast between the old Maxine and this new creature standing before Mrs. Vonk was so great and so pleasing that she could not refrain from commenting. She complimented her on her appearance, ending with, "And your hair! You've trimmed and styled it. Maxine, it's beautiful. I hope you'll always wear it like this."

Maxine gave half a sneer and said, "I should give my mother such satisfaction! My hair has been the bane of her existence for the last eight years and I'm not about to remove that aggravation now. I'm wearing my roommate's wig."

The words sounded cold and hard, but she was serious. The rest of the semester, she wore her hair in its usual state of disarray. Obviously, Maxine was deriving a sadistic pleasure from the thought that she had tortured her mother the past eight years. That's a long time! Much aggravation, many strained moments, and perhaps a legion of harsh, bitter words had passed between mother and daughter over Maxine's unwillingness to keep her hair neatly groomed.

But the question arises whether the situation would have gotten so out of hand if Maxine's mother had ignored her hair eight years ago. It's no fun to tease or torment a person who doesn't respond by showing signs of resentment and irritation. Is it possible for adults to make mountains out of molehills to the extent that the molehill becomes a mountain so huge and so unsurmountable that it develops into a permanent barrier between parent and child?

In Paul's epistle to the Ephesians (4:26), he told them not to let the sun go down on their wrath. In other words, nip any misunderstandings between yourself and others in the bud so you can face each morning assured that God will forgive you because you have forgiven others.

Paul expounds upon the need for us to set our affection on things above, not on things on the earth, if we would be risen with Christ. *(Read Colossians 3:1-17.)*

Intolerance breeds many sins. Self-righteousness is among them. The more prejudices we adopt, the more certain we are that our way of thinking, acting, and living is the best. We become narrow-minded and bigoted by refusing to see the other side of the problem. We cease to seek the truth, and become so opinionated that we are only interested in those who think as we think and agree with our actions.

Barriers between two individuals are always regrettable, but barriers between members of a family are tragic. Once such a barrier is built, it does not remain miniature in size. Instead, every day it is allowed to remain between two friends, mother and daughter, father and son, or any other relationship, it increases in height and width and destiny. Finally the barrier becomes seemingly unsurmountable because neither will admit being wrong.

In such incidents we become like the two small boys, James and Bobby, who were separated because of the violent argument in which they were engaged. Since Bobby seemed at fault, he was sent upstairs to his room to think over the unhappy occurrence . After a few minutes of silence, his mother called to him from below, inquiring as to what he was doing.

"I'm praying," came the prompt reply.

"That's fine, Bobby," his mother assured him. "What are you praying about?"

"I'm praying that God will forgive Jimmy," came the reply, "and make him a good boy like me."

The ancient psalmist wrote, "Behold, how good and how pleasant it is for brethren to dwell together in unity!" *(Psalm 133:1)*. The modern psalmist might write, "Behold how good and how pleasant it is for all members of a family to dwell together in peace and harmony!"

Closing Hymn: Blest Be the Tie That Binds

Closing Thought

May we be big enough to forgive, and compassionate enough to forget when we have been wronged.

May we be courageous enough to beg another's forgiveness, and humble enough to acknowledge a failure when we have wronged.

We seek this benediction in the name of our Lord and Savior, Jesus. Amen.

Strengthening Home Ties

Be ye kind one to another (Ephesians 4:32).

~~~~~~

Opening Meditation

Happiness Through Thoughtfulness

The happiness in every home could be increased
A thousandfold by little courtesies
And simple acts of thoughtfulness
Between members of the family.
A worthwhile goal in life is so to live
That every night before we close our eyes
We truthfully can say,
"Today, through a loving word,
I gave some happiness
To a member of my family.
Today, through a thoughtful act,
I added joy to our home.
Today I showed my family how much I care."

Opening Hymn: I Know Whom I Have Believed

Devotional

Two university men were discussing their favorite topic—girls.

"You're taking *Cathy?*" the first student said, "How come? I thought you'd take Joan."

"No way," the second student said.

"But I thought you and Joan were going steady."

"Not any more."

"How come?"

"She's too neurotic."

"Neurotic? What do you mean?"

"Why, she writes to her mother every week! Imagine writing to your *mother* EVERY WEEK!"

One has to feel sorry for the young man who considered Joan neurotic because she wrote to her mother every week. He has missed something very special in life—a close relationship between a young person and his parents.

During the past two decades, much has been said about the so-called generation gap. Estranged relations between parents and young people in the home not only are accepted as inevitable, but are expected to occur. It would seem that the expression *generation gap* is a misnomer, for what is really meant is a gap in understanding between two individuals, not necessarily of different generations— and such gaps appear constantly outside as well as inside the home. Here was a good example—a gap between two college students—a young lady who obviously kept in close touch with home, and a young man who obviously did not. He considered a healthy relationship between a young lady and her mother a sign of neurosis.

Thomas Jefferson felt that "the happiness of the domestic fireside is the first boon of heaven."

C. W. Parkhurst expressed the same thought: "Home interprets heaven. Home is heaven for beginners."

But family unity cannot exist without close communication between all members. There cannot be half-truths, holding back, or distrust. Conversation, discussion, and the exchange of opinions as well as ideas must be encouraged and practiced by every member of the family in order for meaningful communication to exist.

Mary Catherwood, American writer, in her tale, "Marianson," expresses this thought: "Two may talk together under the same roof for many years, yet never really meet; and two others at first speech are old friends."

Someone has said that lack of communication is the secret of all human sorrow.

And seeing the multitudes Jesus taught them, beginning first with the Beatitudes. Immediately following He said,

Ye are the salt of the earth: but if the salt has lost his savor, wherewith shall it be salted? . . .

Ye are the light of the world. A city that is set on a hill cannot be hid.

Neither do men light a candle, and put it under a bushel, but on a candlestick; and it giveth light unto all that are in the house.

Let your light so shine before men, that they may see your good works, and glorify your Father which is in heaven *(Matthew 5:13-16).*

Jesus reveals here what all who profess to follow Him should be. First, the salt of the earth. Salt flavors. Salt preserves. Salt prevents destruction. Such is the role of a Christian within the home. To flavor the homelife with love and understanding. To preserve harmony and peace. To keep the family unit strong.

Through His words, *the light of the world,* Jesus compares the role of a follower to the sun. As God created the sun to enlighten the world, so Christians are expected to bring light and warmth and happiness to others, beginning with the family circle.

What better way can we glorify God than to let our lights so shine within our homes that through our family relationships we glorify our Father which is in Heaven?

Tolstoy, the Russian novelist, wrote, "All happy families resemble one another; every unhappy family is unhappy in its own way." Surely the reason all happy families resemble one another is that the families' roots are deeply embedded in the teachings of Christ.

Closing Hymn: He Leadeth Me

Closing Thought

Send Thy light into our hearts, dear Lord,
That we may find contentment, peace, and love within our homes.
For where peace and love abide,
There Thou art also.

Little Things Can Make a Big Difference

Thou shalt love the Lord thy God with all thy heart, and with all thy soul, and with all thy mind.
This is the first and great commandment.
And the second is like unto it, Thou shalt love thy neighbor as thyself
(Matthew 22:37-39).

~~~~~~

Opening Meditation

God is love.
When we keep love in our hearts
We keep God there too.
God's love for us
Is far too great to comprehend fully.
But this we understand
That we can best
Reveal our love for God
By demonstrating our love
For our fellow beings.

Opening Hymn: Give Me Thy Heart

Devotional

A keyboard operator was busy preparing programs for pre-holiday activities. For about a week, she had worked extra hours and strained her eyes to get all the copy to the printer on time. One day she had read proof so constantly that by late afternoon her vision was blurry. She didn't trust herself to read proof for the one remaining page of Christmas carols.

A friend happened by just then; so she called to him and asked him to proof the remaining sheet for her. Halfway through, he burst out laughing.

"It's a good thing you asked me to read this page," he said. He pointed to a line that should have read "Sing in exultation," but in the typing, the letter *g* had been omitted from the word *sing!*

What a difference a single letter made in that word! In the meaning of that sentence! Imagine an audience singing joyously "Sin in exultation!"

How often in everyday life, seemingly small, insignificant things can change a situation from something beautiful to something ugly or distasteful. It may be something as small as a sneer, a slur, a word spoken out of turn, a facial expression, or even just a voice intonation. And it can work the other way too. Some small, insignificant thing can change a situation from something ugly or distasteful to something beautiful. A smile, a friendly greeting, a word of encouragement can work wonders.

It is of utmost importance to proofread with care a page before sending it to the printer to be sure the printed copy represents exactly what the writer intended to say. It's just as important to proofread every gesture, spoken word, facial expression and intonation before you send it forth as representative of your real self, or at least the self you are striving to be.

A kind word is seldom spoken in vain. A kind deed is seldom lost.

A prominent doctor was questioned concerning his practice of devoting one full day each week to working in the crowded tenement areas of his city. "Why?" he was constantly asked. "Why are you devoting so much of your valuable time to work for which you receive no pay, when your services are so eagerly sought after by people who would willingly make your time and efforts worthwhile?"

The doctor's reply was always the same. "Years ago, when I was a child, someone was kind to me. That kindness changed my whole life. Without it, I would not be the person I am today. This is the least I can do to express my thanks to someone whose name I do not know."

David Star Jordan, an American biologist and educator, wrote, "Today is your day and mine, the only day we have, the day in which we play our part. What our part may signify in the great whole we may not understand; but we are here to play it, and now is our time. This we know—it is a part of action, not of whining. It is a part of love, not cynicism. It is for us to express love in terms of human helpfulness."

Paul's letters to the newly founded congregations are laden with words of advice and encouragement concerning the importance of attitudes and actions one toward another.

Be kind one to another, tender-hearted, forgiving one another, even as God for Christ's sake hath forgiven you.

Charity suffereth long, and is kind.

Be kindly affectioned one to another with brotherly love; in honor preferring one another (Ephesians 4:32; 1 Corinthians 13:4; Romans 12:10).

In James 1:22-24 we read,

Be ye doers of the word, and not hearers only, deceiving your own selves.

For if any be a hearer of the word, and not a doer, he is like unto a man beholding his natural face in a glass:

For he beholdeth himself, and goeth his way, and straightway forgetteth what manner of man he was.

In 2 Peter 1:5-7, we are given a summary of Christian attributes:

And besides this, giving all diligence, add to your faith virtue; and to virtue, knowledge; and to knowledge, temperance; and to temperance, patience; and to patience, godliness; and to godliness, brotherly kindness; and to brotherly kindness, charity.

William Penn is credited with these words: "I expect to pass through life but once. If, therefore, there be any kindness I can show, or any good thing I can do to any fellow being, let me do it now, and not deter or neglect it, as I shall not pass this way again."

Closing Hymn: Wonderful Savior

Closing Thought

May we never cease giving thanks to God
for His many blessings to us.
Nor to our family and friends
for even the smallest favor or kindness;
For out of the depths of gratitude
comes sincere and lasting love.

Frustration Blocks

The peace of God, which passeth all understanding, shall keep your hearts and minds through Christ Jesus (Philippians 4:7).

~~~~~~

Opening Meditation

Time is so fleeting.
Time is so limited.
Let us find God,
And having found Him,
Let us keep close to His side.
Let us find Him today.
Tomorrow may never dawn for us.
The present moment is all we have to use
Or to waste in the service of God.

Opening Hymn: Sweet Hour of Prayer

Devotional

A woman was searching in a neighbor's garage for something that could be used to make a stone wall for a children's play when she noticed something that caught her eye. On a workbench in the garage was a two-by-four about a yard long with nails driven into it seemingly at random. Some nails had been driven all the way into the wood with such force that final sharp blows left hammer impressions. Other nails were driven in only halfway. Many were at angles and then bent over. There seemed neither pattern nor purpose for the nails; so the lady inquired about them.

"That's my frustration block," the owner of the garage, a school teacher, told her. "Years ago I learned that children respond more quickly to love and understanding than to constant nagging and scolding. That doesn't mean I never get aggravated and frustrated. When I do, I restrain myself in the classroom and come home, straight to my workbench, and take it all out on that two-by-four. Incidentally," she added, "that's my third one! When I take my frustration out on that piece of wood, I can return to the classroom the next day and start right in loving each child—you know, with patience toward all and malice toward none."

Some unknown poet has left us these lines:

It's the little things that nag and needle
Like the sting of wasp or beetle,
But herein lies a paradox
For little things like stones and rocks
Can build a wall or a foundation
That make a man or make a nation.

We're all human. Each of us has a saturation point, and, if pressed beyond that level of aggravation or frustration, unless we have a safety valve, we are apt to lose self-control and say or do something for which we are ashamed, or which we will regret when the aggravation or frustration diminishes.

A good safety valve is prayer. It's better than a two-by-four. It brings instant comforting relief that clears a woman's head, enables her to hold her tongue, and often helps her avert unpleasant happenings.

For regular daily prayers—not those evoked on the spur of the moment out of depths of despair or the pressing need for immediate help—we need a quiet setting and solitude.

Gathering His disciples about Him, Jesus taught them concerning prayer. Jesus said, "When thou prayest, thou shalt not be as the hypocrites are: for they love to pray standing in the synagogue and in the corners of the streets, that they may be seen of men. Verily I say unto you, They have their reward.

"But thou, when thou prayest, enter into thy closet, and when thou hast shut thy door, pray to thy Father which is in secret; and thy Father which seeth in secret shall reward thee openly.

"But when ye pray, use not vain repetitions, as the heathen do; for they think that they shall be heard for their much speaking.

"Be not ye therefore like unto them: for your Father knoweth what things ye have need of, before ye ask him" *(Matthew 6:5-9)*.

One of the most wonderful aspects of prayer is that, in His infinite wisdom, God did not designate a certain time, a certain place, or a certain pattern for prayers. Victor Hugo wrote, "Certain thoughts are prayers. There are moments when, whatever be the attitude of the body, the soul is on its knees." Such moments can be in the classroom with thirty-five children present. They can be in the home of the den mother in the midst of a Brownie or Boy Scout meeting. They can be at the dinner table when one member of the family has had a trying day and returns home filled with aggravation and frustration.

Christina Rosetti, in her *The Face of the Deep,* wrote, "Well spake that soldier who being asked what he would do if he became too weak to cling to Christ, answered, 'Then I will pray Him to cling to me.' "

What a comforting thought! And what a wonderful experience it is to feel Christ clinging to us, lifting us out of the depths of despair or aggravation or frustration and thus transforming bedlam in the class-room, chaos in the home, crises in situations involving others—all through the great and wonderful power of silent prayer.

Closing Hymn: Softly and Tenderly

Closing Thought

They that have faith
Shall renew their strength and hope
Through prayer,
For prayer is the sacred key
That fits the door
Between our souls and God.

Needless Emptiness

Greater love hath no man than this, that a man lay down his life for his friends (John 15:13).

~~~~~~

Opening Meditation

When we truly find the Lord,
Then peace shall dwell within our hearts—
The peace that passes understanding—
The peace that comes with each new dawning—
The peace that stills our troubled souls—
The peace that fills our hearts when we are
Communing with God through prayer.
"My peace I leave wtih you," Christ said.
His peace is ours for the taking.

Opening Hymn: Sweeter as the Years Go By

Devotional

Two elderly ladies were seated at a table facing the front entrance of a restaurant. They were carefully groomed, their nails manicured, and just enough rouge to add a bit of color to their aged, wrinkled cheeks. One of the women looked into the face of every person who came through the front door as though she were looking for someone in particular and was afraid she would not recognize him.

Her companion paid no attention to anyone. She sat looking straight ahead through the glass doors, never bothering to give even a casual glance toward those who came and went.

At length, the first woman sighed and said, "I don't know hardly anybody anymore."

Whereupon the second lady, her gaze still straight ahead, said, "It's been a long time since I've known anybody."

What a tragedy to live day after day not knowing "anybody anymore." Giving up all hope of finding even one familiar face. Ending life in a world of strangers.

Time was when all the members of a family married, settled down, raised a family, and died no farther than fifty miles from their birthplace. Today it is a rarity to find all members of a family residing in the same state.

The more mobile we are, the more we move from place to place, the greater is our need to cultivate new friends wherever we go, and to extend a sincere friendship to newcomers.

As a person grows older, there is a tendency to cling to the past. To be satisfied with the remembrances of friendships now ended by death. To feel reluctant to put forth the required energy needed to cultivate new friends. But the words, "It's been a long time since I've known anybody," makes us keenly aware of how needlessly empty the aged years of our lives can become.

If we live by the teachings of Christ, old age will never be empty, nor will we find ourselves strangers in the world in which we have lived many years.

Give, and it shall be given unto you; good measure, pressed down, and shaken together, and running over, shall men give into your bosom. For with the same measure that ye mete withal it shall be measured to you again *(Luke 6:38)*.

Those who give much of themselves through service, through friendship, through caring for others will reap the blessings from the giving of such love in their old age.

The seeds of friendship, planted in youth and nurtured throughout life, will bring rich harvest—pressed down and running over—at the time in life when friends, both old and new, are one of life's richest blessings.

"He alone has lost the art to live who cannot win new friends." These words of S. Wier Mitchell are not only words of caution; they are words of encouragement and challenge. Surrounded by friends, as we grow older, we can feel as Elizabeth Cady Stanton expressed it so well:

Having gleefully chased butterflies in our young days on our way to school, we thought it might be as well to chase them in our old age on the way to heaven.

Closing Hymn: Jesus, Lover of My Soul

Closing Thought

It is not by the gray of the hair that one knows the age of the heart—*Bulwer.*

Self-Confidence

*Be watchful, stand firm in your faith, be courageous, be strong. Let
all that you do be done in love (1 Corinthians 16:13, 14 RSV).*

∿∿∿∿∿∿∿∿∿∿∿∿∿∿∿∿∿∿∿∿∿∿∿∿∿∿∿

Opening Meditation
Respect Through Self-Respect
Self-respect does not mean self-conceit,
Or boastful egotism,
Or exaggerated opinions of oneself.
Self-respect means the ability
To lift one's head and hold it high with pride
For what an individual has achieved
Through service rendered to a fellow man,
Or through the strength of Christian character
Developed by the daily practicing of truth,
Sincerity, self-discipline, benevolence, and honesty.
Self-respect is like a flashing beacon light
Whose gleaming arc is seen on every side for miles.
When one has earned his self-respect, it radiates
About him like a silent, brilliant beacon light,
Demanding, on its own, respect from fellow men.

Opening Hymn: Guide Me, O Thou Great Jehovah

Devotional
Parent-teacher conferences are scheduled in many school sys-
tems. Children are granted a one-day vacation each semester, free-
ing the teacher for brief, private sessions with parents of the children
in her class. Teachers often take advantage of the first of such conference days to meet with the parents of any so-called "problem"
children.

The word "problem" might refer to a weak academic area, a
suspected visual or auditory deficiency, a child too advanced for his
group, a child with outstanding talent, or a behavior or emotional
problem.

Jamie was not a behavior problem, at least not in Mrs. Vonk's
class. He was repeating the second grade, but was off to a good start.
Mrs. Vonk felt that if his mother would cooperate and follow her

suggestions for helping him at home, he could easily be performing on an average second-grade level before Christmas; on a high second-grade level by spring.

Since all past parent-teacher conferences had been to inform Jamie's mother of his poor performance and his lack of self-discipline, she expected the worst when she received Mrs. Vonk's note requesting an appointment for the first conference day. As she entered the classroom and walked briskly from the door to the teacher's desk, she said in a voice that matched her lively step, "Good morning, Mrs. Vonk. What can I do to help my poor, slow, stupid child?"

It took Mrs. Vonk a moment to recover, and by that time Jamie's mother had eased gracefully into the chair by her desk and sat waiting for a reply.

"But Jamie is not a poor, slow, stupid child," Mrs. Vonk began.

With a wave of her hand, Jamie's mother interrupted. "Mrs. Vonk, don't try to spare me. I got through college by the skin of my teeth, and heaven knows his father's no brain!"

It was no easy task for Mrs. Vonk to convince Jamie's mother that all Jamie needed was love and encouragement. Given a fair chance to develop his self-ego at home as well as at school, he had the ability to achieve.

Whether we are aware of it or not, we are constantly transmitting our innermost feelings to those about us. Parent to child. Child to parent. Child to child. Adult to adult. Friend to friend. Stranger to stranger. We are transmitting our confidence or our lack of complete trust. Our concern or our indifference. Our love or our contempt. Our understanding or our intolerance. Such transmissions either aid or destroy another's self-confidence; and self-esteem, according to F. M. Colley, "is the most valuable of the emotions." For, to quote R. W. Clark, "no external advantage can supply the place of self-reliance."

Thoreau reminds us, "Men were born to succeed, not to fail," but until the individual develops self-confidence and self-esteem, he will lack the incentive to put forth his best efforts. "There is no use whatever trying to help people who do not try to help themselves," wrote Andrew Carnegie. "You cannot push anyone up a ladder unless he is willing to climb." J. G. Holland expressed the same thought. "God gives every bird his food, but does not throw it into the nest."

Perhaps the greatest obstacle in combating our lack of self-

106

confidence or attempting to help someone else overcome her lack of self-confidence is that we try to achieve what seems the impossible without God's help.

"With God all things are possible *(Matthew 19:26)*. . . . If thou canst believe, all things are possible to him that believeth *(Mark 9:23)*. . . . With men it is impossible, but not with God: for with God all things are possible *(Mark 10:27)*. . . . The things which are impossible with men are possible with God" *(Luke 18:27)*.

On one occasion, Jesus stressed the value of every individual in the sight of God when He told His disciples, "Are not two sparrows sold for a farthing? and one of them shall not fall on the ground without your Father. But the very hairs of your head are all numbered. Fear ye not therefore, ye are of more value than many sparrows *(Matthew 10:29-31)*.

Alone we can do little; with God's help, we can accomplish much.

Closing Hymn: Revive Us Again

Closing Thought

Margaret Chase Smith, the first woman to be elected to both the House of Representatives and the Senate, wrote the following words:

This I Believe

I believe that in our constant search for security we can never gain any peace of mind until we secure our own soul. And this I do believe above all, especially in my times of greater discouragement, *that I must believe*—that I must believe in my fellow men—that I must believe in myself—that I must believe in God—if life is to have any meaning.

Here Lies a Christian

The gift of God is eternal life through Jesus Christ our Lord (Romans 6:23).

~~~~~~

Opening Meditation

Strait is the gate
And narrow the way
That leads to eternal life.
Jesus said,
I am the way,
the truth, and
the life.
May we ceaselessly strive to follow Jesus,
humbly—with open hearts;
meekly—with open minds;
lowly—with open eyes;
For no one cometh unto the Father
But by Him.

Opening Hymn: Where He Leads Me

Devotional

It's always interesting to read the inscriptions on tombstones, especially those located in old cemeteries. The following inscription could have been entitled, "Here Lies a Christian." It is from a grave stone in the historic cemetery at Midway, Georgia, and was inscribed before the War Between the States.

Sacred
to the Memory of
John Stacy, Esq.
Born Dec. 10, 1761   Died April 7, 1818
He was of manners, simple & dignified,
of disposition, mild & even;
not censorious of the conduct of others,
scrupulous, of his own;
dispassionate in adopting his opinions,
steady in maintaining them.
His religion was without ostentation,

his zeal without bigotry.
his friendship without pretence;
These were less discovered in his word than actions.
Ostensibly adicted to no vice,
not wanting in any virtue,
he established a character, &
in the circle in which he moved,
unassailable by malevolence,
untarnished by reproach.
In matters of moment, he was wont to be chosen
a Counsellor;
in cases of doubtful & disputed right,
an Arbiter.
in feuds & contentions of party,
a Peacemaker,
inflexible in his integrity as
a Civil Magistrate;
grave in deportment, as becomes
a Deacon:
examplary in all the relations of life as
a Christian.

Yes, this inscription could have been entitled, "Here Lies a Christian." Although John Stacy, Esq. died at the age of fifty-six, it would appear that he had lived a life of service to God, to his family, and to his fellow citizens. Surely his loss would have been keenly felt by many, but he left this world well prepared for the next. Tyron Edwards noted, "A faithful Christian life in this world is the best preparation for the next."

To most of us, regardless of age, death seems too far in the future to give much thought to the meaning of passing from this life to the next. We feel comfortable and comforted with the promises of Christ concerning our future life.

Let not your heart be troubled: ye believe in God, believe also in me.

In my Father's house are many mansions: if it were not so, I would have told you. I go to prepare a place for you.

And if I go and prepare a place for you, I will come again, and receive you unto myself; that where I am, there ye may be also (John 14:1-3).

And this is the record, that God hath given to us eternal life, and this life is in his Son.

He that hath the Son hath life; and he that hath not the Son of God hath not life *(1 John 5:11, 12)*.

Concerning death, N. Macleod wrote, "We picture death as coming to destroy; let us rather picture Christ as coming to save. We think of death as ending; let us rather think of life as beginning, and that more abundantly. We think of losing; let us think of gaining. We think of parting; let us think of meeting. We think of going away; let us think of arriving. And as the voice of death whispers, 'You must go from earth,' let us hear the voice of Christ saying, 'You are but coming to Me.' "

A family suddenly became concerned about seven-year-old Susie, the only child in a family of adults. All the oldsters agreed among themselves to do their part in educating Susie as to the meaning of death, as most of them were well along in years, and certainly Susie would outlive all of them, barring some tragic accident.

So, at appropriate times when alone with Susie, each uncle, aunt, and grandparent explained death to Susie in his or her own way. One Sunday noon the phone rang while the family was gathered around the lunch table. The grandmother of Susie's friend down the street had been very ill, and the call was from Betsy telling Susie her grandmother had just passed away. Susie returned to the table, glowing, and declared with much feeling, "Betsy's grandmother just died! That lucky duck!"

Perhaps the oldsters of Susie's family had over-educated Susie for the passing of one of them—or had they? What a wonderful attitude to take. That lucky duck! Betsy's grandmother was now enjoying the happiness of eternal life, just as Christ had promised.

Closing Hymn: In the Sweet By and By

Biographical Index

Addams, Jane (1860-1935). Am. Social worker, founder of Hull House.
Addison, Joseph (1672-1719). Eng. essayist and poet.
Antrim, Minna (1861-?). Am. writer.
Aster, Lady Nancy (1879-1964). Eng. politician, first woman to sit in British House of Commons.

Barton, Bruce (1886-?). Am. author.
Beecher, Henry Ward (1813-1887). Am. clergyman and reformer.
Bok, Edward (1863-1930). Am. journalist.
Bond, Carrie Jacobs (1862-1946). Am. songwriter and composer.
Bowen, Francis (1811-1890). Am. philosopher.
Branch, Anna Hempstead (1875-1937). Am. poet and social worker.
Brisbane, Arthur (1864-1936). Am. journalist.
Brooks, Phillips (1835-1893). Am. clergyman.
Brown, Chas. F. (1834-1867). Am. humorist.
Bryant, William Cullen (1794-1878). Am. poet and editor.
Bulwer-Lytton, Edward George (1803-1873). Eng. politician and novelist.
Burke, Edmund (1729-1797). Eng. statesman.
Byron, Lord George Gordon (1788-1824). Eng. poet.

Carnegie, Andrew (1835-1919). Scot. Am. capitalist and philanthropist.
Carney, Julia (1823-1908). Am. educator and poet.
Catherwood, Mary (1874-1901). Am. writer.
Cavell, Edith Louisa (1865-1915). Eng. nurse and patriot.
Cecil, Richard (1748-1777). Eng. clergy.
Clark, R. W. (1813-1886). Am. clergy.
Colley, F. M. (fl. 1850). Am. clergy.
Coolidge, Calvin (1872-1933). 30th U.S. President.
Cowper, William (1731-1800). Eng. poet.
Craker, Wendel D. (?). Contemporary clergy and educator.

Dickinson, Emily (1830-1886). Am. poet.
Dunning, W. E. (1812-1876). Am. clergy and writer.

Edwards, Tyron (1809-1894). Am. theologian and editor.
Eliot, George (1819-1880). Pseud. Mary Ann Evans Cross, Eng. novelist.
Emerson, Ralph Waldo (1803-1882). Am. poet and essayist.
Everett, Edward (1794-1865). Am. statesman and orator.
Everton, John (fl. 1850). Am. clergy

Franklin, Benjamin (1706-1790). Am. statesman, author, inventor
Fuller, Margaret (1810-1850). Am. author.

Garrison, Theodosia (1874-1944). Am. poet and writer.
Goethe, Johann Wolfgang von (1749-1832). Ger. poet, dram., philos.
Grothingham, O. L. (fl. 1850). Am. clergy and writer.

Hall, E. B. (fl. 1850). Am. clergy.
Hamilton, Gail (1833-1896). Am. writer and humorist.

Heathon, Henrietta (1825-1915). Eng. writer and poet.
Holland, J. G. (1819-1881). Am. author.
Horne, George (1730-1792). Eng. clergy.
Howard, John (1726-1790). Eng. prison reformer.
Hubbard, Elbert (1859-1915). Am. author and lecturer.
Hubbard, Kin (Frank) (1868-1930). Am. humorist.
Hugo, Victor (1802-1885). Fr. author.

Jefferson, Thomas (1743-1826). 3rd U.S. President.
Jordan, David Starr (1851-1931). Am. biologist and educator.

Keller, Helen Adams (1880-1968). Am. writer and lecturer. Blind and deaf
    from early childhood.
Kingsley, Charles (1819-1875). Eng. clergy and novelist.

Lind, Jenny (1820-1887). Swed. opera singer.
Lorimer, George (1868-?). Am. editor.
Lowell, James R. (1819-1891). Am. poet and essayist.
Luther, Martin (1483-1546). Ger. religious reformer.

Macleod, Norman (1812-1872). Scot. clergy.
Marquis, Don (1878-1937). Am. journalist and humorist.
Mason, James (1706-1773). Am. clergy.
McCreedy, John L. (1836-1906). Am. journalist and poet.

Simmons, Charles (1798-1856). Am. clergy and litterateur.
Simons, William D. (?). 18th cent. Am. clergy.
Smith, Margaret Chase (1897-   ). Am. congresswoman, first woman
    elected to both House of Representatives and Senate.
South, Robert (1634-1716). Eng. clergy.
Southey, Robert (1774-1843). Eng. poet laureate.
Stanton, Elizabeth Cady (1815-1902). Am. suffragist and writer.
Stevenson, Robert Louis (1850-1894). Scot. author.
Sullivan, Annie (1866-1936). Am. educator of deaf and blind. Helen Keller's
    teacher.

Taylor, Jeremy (1613-1667). Eng. clergy.
Teasdale, Sara (1884-1933). Am. poet.
Tennyson, Alfred, Lord (1809-1892). Eng. poet laureate.
Thoreau, H. D. (1817-1862). Am. naturalist and essayist.
Tolstoy, Leo (1828-1910). Russ. author.
Trumbull, H. C. (1830-1903). Am. clergy.
Twain, Mark (1835-1910). Real name: Clemens, Samuel, Am. humorist and
    writer.

Washington, George (1732-1799). First U.S. President.
Watson, Thomas (died about 1690). Eng. clergy.
Webster, Daniel (1782-1852). Am. orator and statesman.
Wells, M. M. (?) 19th cent. clergy and hymn writer.
Wesley, Charles (1707-1788). Eng. organist and composer.
Whittier, John Greenleaf (1807-1892). Am. poet.